AF251654

WHAT? AGAIN THOSE JEWS!

HENRY L. LANTNER

WHAT? AGAIN THOSE JEWS!

HENRY L. LANTNER

Copyright © H.L. Lantner & Gefen Publishing House
Jerusalem 1997/5757

All rights reserved. No part of this publication may be translated,
reproduced, stored in a retrieval system or transmitted, in any form
or by any means, electronic, mechanical, photocopying, recording or
otherwise, without express written permission from the publishers.

Typesetting: Marzel A.S. – Jerusalem

Cover Design: Gil Friedman / Gefen

ISBN 965-229-158-7

Edition 9 8 7 6 5 4 3 2 1

Gefen Publishing House Ltd.   Gefen Books
POB 36004, Jerusalem   12 New St., Hewlett
91360 Israel   N.Y., U.S.A. 11557
972-2-5380247   516-295-2805

Printed in Israel

Send for our free catalogue

To those who deny their Jewishness,

and to all others who defy it

Contents

Author's Note

When my children were still small, I was often asked to perform the pleasant duty of reading bed-time stories to them, until they fell asleep. This habit of reading stories continued even when the children grew older. But in later years, whenever any of the narratives became boring and failed to hold their attention, I would revert to telling them some of my own stories, instead. These "true" stories, as they were called by my children, I would draw freely from my numerous encounters and experiences in various foreign countries. And when the children grew up, they often returned to their suggestion – or should I say insistence – that I publish some of those stories in the form of a book. My children thought they were of wide interest and possessed moral implications.

Thus, one day, I decided to go through the various files I keep in my desk drawer. On close examination of the accumulated material, I discovered that whenever any of the stories touched on the subject of Jews and Judaism, they nearly always revealed a critical, insulting and hostile attitude towards Jews. Hence, my decision to write this book against anti-Semitism. In it, I set out to unfold and disprove many of the baseless allegations, devious claims, and false charges made against the Jewish people.

H.L.L.

Acknowledgments

This is a personal interpretation of the nature and history of Christian anti-Semitism. The opinions expressed and illustrations used are my own. But my debt to many scholars, both Jewish and non-Jewish, who illuminated my understanding of this exceptionally vexed problem, will be evident to anyone who looks at the sources listed at the end of the book. However, to Professor Alan M. Dershowitz of Harvard University, prominent lawyer and well-known defender of individual rights, particular gratitude is due for his uncompromising stand against anti-Semitism, anti-Zionism, and racism. In this connection, he expresses strong beliefs and views on the question of being a proud and assertive Jew, lucidly expounded in his book *Chutzpah*. To the Vidal Sassoon International Center for the Study of Anti-Semitism at The Hebrew University, Jerusalem, I am grateful for examining the manuscript, and expressing their appreciation for my interest in the study of anti-Semitism, and its religious and popular roots. Thanks are also due to the editors of the *Encyclopedia Judaica* and *The Encyclopedia of Judaism,* which proved to be indispensable guides to events and landmarks in the history of the Jewish people.

I am also indebted to the following: my daughter, Revital
Lantner-Fuchs, for overseeing the production of the
manuscript through all its stages, my editors at Gefen
Publishing House, Jerusalem, and the firm's directors, Messrs.
Ilan and Dror Greenfield, for publishing this book.

Utterances of an Anti-Semite

"I am not against the Jews just because they are Jews, but because they are greedy, wear side-curls, speak Yiddish, and don't want to assimilate, but also because they assimilate, stop speaking Yiddish, dress smartly, and want to be gentiles. Because they are uncultured, and because they are too much cultured. Because they are backward, superstitious and ignorant, and because they are exceptionally clever, progressive, and ambitious. Because they have long aquiline noses, and because it is often difficult to tell them from 'pure' Aryans. Because they crucified Jesus, practise religious slaughter and pore over the Talmud, but also because they reject their own religion, and become atheists. Because they are skinny, unhealthy, and born cowards, and because they practice sports, are aggressive, and have a lot of cheek. Because they are bankers and capitalists, and because they are communists and Zionists. But I am definitely not against them just because they are Jews."

K.A. Jelenski, *HANBA CZY WSTYD* (Disgrace or Shame), translated from the original Polish.

Twenty Centuries of Unabated Anti-Semitism as Expressed Through Various Accusations

For almost two thousand years Christian anti-Semitism served directly and indirectly as a primary and fundamental cause of widespread hatred against Jews. This was so in the early days of the Church, the medieval period and even in our secular times.

With the passage of time, anti-Semitism moved from its predominantly religious context to social, political and economic spheres. Although the various charges levelled at the Jews show a tendency to change in content during the centuries, they do retain their malicious character and purpose, throughout the different periods of Christian history.

During the Early Church Period, the Jews were denounced as: Christ killers, Christ rejectionists, followers of anti-Christ, agents of anti-Christ, infidels, host wafer desecrators, Sodom and Gomora sinners, godless pagans, heretics, Judases, eternal wanderers, mankind's enemies, an accursed people, a useless race, sinful creatures, outcasts, demons, satans, vampires, secret killers, ritual murderers.

During the Medieval Church Period, the Jews were branded as: God murderers, infidels, well poisoners, barbarians, parasites, rascals, bribers, degenerates, sorcerers, oppressors, sadists, usurers, bloodsuckers, devils, magicians, slaves, primitives, superstitious, malevolent, corrupt, immoral, homeless wanderers, seditious, sexually wicked, loathsome, and contemptible.

During the Early Secular Period, the Jews were portrayed as: nomads, strangers, intruders, clannish, isolationist, imbeciles, vulgar, aggressive, stubborn, cruel, vengeful, decadent, rogues, villains, fanatics, repugnant, abominable, superstitious narrow-minded, hypocrites, exploiters, egotists, tricky, money worshippers, unscrupulous moneylenders, dishonest and greedy.

During the Modern Period, the Jews have been labelled as: outsiders, inferiors, arrogant, domineering, shrewd, fraudulent manipulators, cosmopolitan, unpatriotic, bourgeois, atheists, capitalists, imperialists, fascists, communists, bolsheviks, mensheviks, liberals, pacifists, traitors, Zionists, crypto-Zionists, subversives, revolutionaries, revisionists, racists, freemasons.

In view of such an overwhelming number and variety of wicked allegations, the question arises: How is it possible that people, any people at all, could be collectively accused of such demonic, derogatory, and harmful charges? Yet, throughout the centuries, the Jews alone have been singled out and charged by Christians with embodying such grievous, discriminatory, and totally negative characteristics. However, even a superficial examination of this incomplete list of accusations will readily reveal that some accusations are obviously groundless, false and clearly contradictory. But all of them, without exception, show a strong bias and a blind prejudice, coupled with extreme hatred of the Jewish people. And so, it is hoped that some of the narratives that make up this book will demonstrate and prove again and again the tendentiousness of these wild, utterly hostile allegations, to show them to be deliberately deceptive and totally false. This applies especially to some of the more notorious and widely circulated accusations which, unfortunately, are still propagated and accepted by a great many Christians the world over.

Introduction

Surely, one would not expect a young boy of eight fully to grasp the social and moral implications of anti-Semitism. Yet, this was precisely the age at which, for the very first time, I realized the exact meaning of Jew-hatred. It came about during a "dispute" over religious matters with my Christian pal next door, when I told him that Jesus was a man and a Jew. My claim must have caused him deep resentment for, looking down at me, he retorted angrily: "Don't be stupid! How is it possible for a man to be God. God is invisible and dwells in heaven?" And further, "How could He ever have been Jewish when our religion is totally against the Jews?"

"I don't know," I answered, "but what I do know is that Jesus was a man and a Jew. If you don't believe me, let us go and ask your mother; I am sure she knows."

We ran to see my pal's mother. However, when asked if it was true that Jesus was a Jew, she shrugged her shoulders and would not or could not give us a straightforward answer. All she said was: "We Christians have our God and the Jews have theirs." Reprimanding us for bothering her with such "silly" questions, she turned to us and said: "Why don't the pair of you just go on playing, instead of arguing about matters children should not discuss at all." Greatly disappointed, we left her without resolving our "dispute."

To my luck, while we were still arguing the point outside the house, a monk appeared unexpectedly at the gate of our yard. Dressed in a long brown cassock, he wore sandals but no socks despite the winter. Hanging on his chest was a big wooden cross. I should explain, perhaps, that in our part of Poland, it was customary for monks to visit Christian households every so often to collect money for the upkeep of their monasteries. "Now," I said to my pal, "let us go and ask him. Surely he is the right person to resolve our dispute." Somewhat bashfully we approached the monk and asked him to clarify the matter. Surprised, he looked at us for a moment, and then said in a fatherly voice: "Of course, children, Jesus was a Jew. But why do you ask? Have you any doubts as to His Jewishness?"

"Oh, no, not exactly," answered my chum. "We just wanted to be certain about it."

"Well, now that you know who Jesus was," said the monk, "I am sure you won't forget to say your prayers every morning, and evening before going to bed."

Parting, the monk also gave each of us a holy medal. Before I had time to utter a single word, my pal suddenly disappeared, as if the earth had swallowed him up. Afterwards, he would not speak to me for half a year or so. To this very day, I don't know whether my childhood pal was cross with me because Jesus was a Jew, or because I was right and he was wrong.

Another somewhat similar incident occurred in later years, during World War II, when I arrived in Scotland with a group of freshly enlisted Polish soldiers. We had left what was then the Soviet Union. Our aim was to train with nationals of other armies, as part of the future Allied Expeditionary Forces, preparing for the invasion of Europe. For reasons of maximum security and secrecy about the nature of our training, we were sent to a camp near a small, remote village in the north of Scotland. Apart from radio, contact by other means with the rest of the country was rather limited, since letters and newspapers would reach us only twice, occasionally three times a week. Once, early in the evening, we went back to our living quarters, as usual, following an exceptionally hard and exhausting day of training. Suddenly, without any warning, our door opened wide and an agitated soldier landed in the middle of our barracks. Holding a newspaper in his hand, he called out in excitement: "Listen fellows! Listen to what happened!" At first we thought that perhaps the Germans had already landed on the coast of Britain or, perhaps, some other misfortune had struck the country. But all the greatly excited soldier came to tell us was: "Sarah, the daughter of Mr. Churchill, has secretly married some Jewish bastard from Austria." There was silence for a moment which I broke by shouting back from the other end of the barracks: "Congratulations! Now that I am sort of related to Mr. Churchill through this marriage, could it be that my request for a transfer to the Jewish Brigade will finally be approved?"

In this connection, I should explain that anti-Semitism in the Polish army, as well as among the civilian population, was always present; only its form and intensity varied, according to changing political or economic conditions. But in Britain, during World War II, it was temporarily suppressed, dormant for two reasons. Firstly, because British, and even more so, world public opinion would not easily tolerate it. And secondly, because the greatly inflated number of officers in proportion to ordinary servicemen in our army, favored the benign treatment of each and every soldier, even if he happened to be Jewish. This was the position until the Allied Forces invaded Europe. But after some time, when the first German prisoners-of-war were brought over to Britain, it turned out that quite a sizable proportion of them were actually Poles from Silesia and Pomerania, who had volunteered for service in the German army. Some of them had even joined the notorious S.S. units, as testified by the Nazi swastika, tattooed under their left upper arm. When interrogated, however, they claimed to be Polish citizens and, strangely enough, without much ado, were eagerly accepted into the Polish army.

It goes without saying that the inclusion of those ex-German soldiers into our ranks greatly reinforced the numerical strength of the army. At the same time, it caused hitherto dormant anti-Semitism to flare up again, with even greater intensity than in the past. So much so that, after a short time, a group of two hundred Jewish servicemen declared their unwillingness to continue serving in the Polish Forces. When the matter leaked out in the local press, the military authorities tried hard to hush up the whole affair, but without much success. Eventually, the intervention of the late Professor Harold Lasky, then a Labor member of the British Parliament, resulted in their transfer to the British army. Unfortunately, a number of Jewish soldiers, including myself, serving in various units of the Polish Forces, scattered throughout the British Isles, had intentionally not been informed of the proposed transfer. Much to our regret, we continued to serve in the Polish army practically to the very end of the war.

These two incidents, out of many other similar personal experiences described later, illustrate how deeply anti-Semitic feelings are rooted in Christian society. Characteristically, they also show, as in the case of my young friend, but especially his mother, a total ignorance of some basic facts concerning the Jewish roots of the Christian religion. This ignorance is by no means accidental. It is the result of intentional and prolonged indoctrination of Church and school as part of their reponsibility for Christian religious teachings and education. Instead of presenting the facts, that the Old Testament belongs to both Jews and Christians, that Abraham was our common father, and that Jesus and his mother were Jewish, they try, as far as possible, to suppress and often minimize the connection between Judaism and Christianity. On the other hand, they place a disproportionally widespread emphasis and interpretation on the negative elements of this connection. This is tendentious, and in the majority of cases, unfounded. The result is that, unlike the middle and higher echelons of Christian society, ordinary people know little or nothing of the unbiased truth about the Jews and Judaism.

As a young man, whenever confronted with an abusive allusion or comment about my Jewishness, I would usually retort with some remark, pretending it did not hurt me at all, instead of ignoring it altogether as was expected of me. As I grew old enough to know better, I came to the conclusion that such a response is erroneous and counterproductive, especially now that I have undertaken to write about it in an analytical manner. To the reader, who may suspect me of being over-sensitive about the issue, I would suggest looking up the definition of the word "Jew" in the following: "The Shorter Oxford Dictionary 1987 edition, Webster's Third International English Dictionary 1986 edition, and The Cambridge

Encyclopaedia 1990 edition. A comparison of the definitions of the word "Jew" in the different dictionaries will readily reveal which is derogatory and insulting, and which is fair and balanced. In The Cambridge Encyclopaedia, the entry for "Jew" or "Jewish religion" is left out altogether, despite the fact that entries for some other nations or religions do appear in it. Is this because over four thousand years of Jewish history are not an item important enough to be included, or is it simply because sheer business expediency dictated that the editors of the encyclopaedia to leave it out as a matter of convenience, and include only an entry on modern Israel instead?

My feeling of resentment is even more enhanced in the light of the fact that the contribution of Jews to humanity and the continuous progress and well-being of the civilized world has been enormous. This contribution begins in ancient times with the Old Testament, its Prophets, Judges, and Sages; the philosophers, the poets the scholars, the writers, and the physicians of the Middle Ages. In more recent times it encompasses scientists, inventors, statesmen, composers, musicians, and members of all learned professions. Indeed, the diversity and number of Jews engaged in all those occupations throughout the centuries has been impressive by any standards. To give only one example: Jewish Nobel Prize winners, representing many nations, are a majority both in the Arts and the Sciences. And this is in spite of the fact that, during almost two thousand years, Jews have suffered religious persecution, blood libels, murderous pogroms, social and economic boycotts, and not so very long ago, the worst calamity of all, mass extermination by the Nazis. Now, if that is the case, surely every conscientious, honest, and fair-minded person should ask this question: What is it that makes the Jew an object of such harmful, derogatory, insulting, and hostile attitudes? Anxious to find out a true, logical, and unbiased answer to this exceptionally vexed question myself, I decided to read as many books on the subject as I possibly could get hold of. I searched out books by both Jewish and non-Jewish authors. Now, for the benefit of all those who could not or would not take the trouble to do so themselves, here is the gist of what I learned about this subject:

Anti-Semitism, or more precisely Christian anti-Semitism, springs from the very fact that Jews have not accepted Jesus as their Messiah and as God. And in spite of all the resulting persecutions and sufferings, they managed to survive, sometimes even prosper individually. This obstinate and determined survival of the Jewish people contradicts Christian teachings, that the Church is the true heir to divine promises made to the Children of Israel. Historically, Christian anti-Semitism began in the New Testament, particularly in the gospels of St. Matthew and St. John, with their repeated use of the term "the Jews" in a derogatory and insulting manner.

The real, more modern basis for anti-Semitism, however, and the Church's hostile opposition to Jews returning to their ancestral homeland, lies in an ongoing animosity and contempt for the Jewish people. This negative attitude towards Judaism, perpetuated by the Church throughout the centuries, goes back to the founding Fathers of the Church, but particularly to the early theologians, such as Justin, Augustine, and Chrysostom. They taught, among other things, that Jewish dispersion and suffering are the result of the Jews' rejection of Jesus and, therefore, they must be kept in perpetual degradation, as living witnesses to the truth of Christianity. Consequently, the Land of Israel should be rendered a desert and Jews forbidden forever to return to their homeland.

As a result of this overall condemnation of the Jewish people and Judaism by the Founding Fathers of the Church, successive popes, cardinals, bishops and priests, who began overt anti-Semitic acts, firmly believed that by their various actions, they were carrying true Christian doctrine. Anti-Semitism in Europe, then, was virtually always Church-inspired and initiated. Often, Jews were rounded up and forced to listen to sermons intended to convert them. In addition, they were accused of ritual murders of Christian children, thereby inciting the masses to kill Jews in revenge. It was also the Church that initiated the expulsion of Jews from various cities and villages throughout medieval Europe. In 1347, they were falsely accused of poisoning water wells with the object of spreading the epidemic known as the Black Death. This brought about a widespread massacre of many innocent Jews throughout Europe. Forcible baptism of Jews, and then the hunting down of those practicing Judaism resulted in torture and death by burning during the Spanish and Portuguese Inquisitions. All this and many, many other acts of cruel persecution and physical harm throughout the centuries, provided a fertile ground for the Holocaust, the most inhuman and gigantic crime of all time. Over six million innocent Jewish men, women, and children were brutally murdered.

The hostile attitude of the Catholic Church towards the Jews and Judaism persisted well into the Second World War. Prior to that, there were virtually no serious attempts by the Church either to amend or modify its position. However, two significant events had taken place that brought about a change in the Christian attitude. One was the Holocaust, and the other the establishment of the Jewish state. With regard to the first event, the Catholic Church realized that centuries of biased indoctrination has contributed to a climate in which the Holocaust became possible. During the following decades, this led to some basic revisions of Christian thinking on the subject of anti-Semitism, especially in the Catholic, but also in some of the Protestant Churches. For the Catholic Church, the turning point came with the adoption of the *Nostra Aetate*, or the declaration by the Second Vatican Council in October 1965 on the relations of the Church to Non-Christian Religions. Abandoning the long-held responsibility of the entire Jewish people for the death of Jesus, it started a process of removing anti-Jewish teachings from the Catholic prayers and textbooks, ceased its missions of converting Jews to Christianity, condemned anti-Semitism, and promoted Christian-Jewish relations throughout the world. Protestant Churches also adopted a similar policy. Due to the lack of a monolithic structure like that of the Catholic Church, the attitude of Protestants to the problem is in some respects different. For instance, not all Protestant groups have given up their missionary aim of converting Jews to Christianity, and certain Protestant factions still maintain that there is no role for the Jews in the Christian Divine scheme, because of the rejection of Jesus as the Messiah and as God.

The second event, the establishment of the State of Israel, proved to be an even more serious obstacle in the Jewish-Christian dialogue. Jews all over the world regard the recognition of Israel to be of supreme importance in Jewish self-determination. However, the Roman Catholic Church's attitude for nearly fifty years was negative as regards officially recognizing the State of Israel. This negative attitude was said to have been based on political and pragmatic considerations, chiefly vis-a-vis the Muslim world. But there was a suspicion that theological reasons might also have been involved. Nevertheless, following the Israeli-Palestinian peace accord, and as a result of prolonged negotiations, the Holy See and the State of Israel finally established diplomatic relations on June 15, 1994. Many Protestant Churches, however, still tend to be highly critical of Israel's policies, while the doctrine of denying the Jews any role in the Christian Divine scheme also affects their attitude. Evangelical Churches, on the other hand, have been highly supportive of Israel. Their support is connected with the return of Jews to the Promised Land, which is in accordance with their religious belief, and also because they have strong hopes of eventual Jewish conversion to Christianity. This, then, is a very short profile of Christian-Jewish relations during almost two thousand years of an extremely turbulent and tragic history.

* * *

The subject of anti-Semitism – *one of the longest known hatreds in human history* – has also produced a significant number of books, by both Jewish and non-Jewish writers, especially after the Holocaust. While most of these books in English are thoroughly researched and well written, they seem to suffer from two disadvantages. One is that, being more in the nature of scientific studies, they tend to deal with the subject mostly from the historical perspective, making little or no reference to contemporary developments. The other, even more important, disadvantage is that as such, they are read by a comparatively limited number of people, mostly intellectuals, or those who have a special interest in the subject.

It is mainly for the above reasons that I decided to base this book not so much on the past history of anti-Semitism – though I do refer to it whenever relevant or necessary – as on factual cases in more recent times. In a selection of short accounts, connected mainly, though not exclusively, with my own personal encounters and experiences, I demonstrate the fallacy of many stereotyped and often contradictory accusations made against the Jewish people. Arranged according to various countries I visited during my travels, the stories reveal some of the characteristic expressions of feelings, thoughts, and opinions voiced by different nationals. Among others, they include utterances of such diverse people as a Polish housewife, a Russian manager, an Uzbek engineer, a Scottish colonel, an Irish landlady, as well as the views of many, many others. In this connection, I think, it is important to stress that all those people I came across lived in different countries came from various walks of life, and never met. Therefore, they could not possibly have had anything in common concerning origin, character, background, or culture. Nevertheless, as my narratives reveal, with the exception of one or two instances, they all shared one single sentiment, traced to their common religious roots, namely: their negative attitude towards the Jews and Judaism. It is this universal character of anti-Semitism that prompted me to write about it, and unfold many of its baseless allegations, devious claims, and false charges.

* * *

To address the problem of anti-Semitism mainly, though not only, to western readers, and more specifically to those in Anglo-Saxon countries, the first edition of this book is published in English. And so, while I sincerely hope that all the stories included in it about different people, their backgrounds, national characteristics, and attitudes towards the Jews will be of interest to both Jewish and non-Jewish readers, it is the non-Jewish reader with whom I am particularly concerned. To be more specific, my concern extends to all those non-Jewish readers who, during their lifetime, never came face to face with a Jew but, nevertheless, often claim to know what a Jew is, or rather what he or she are expected to be like, according to their own preconceived notions and ideas.

1 Experiences Of A Jewish Soldier As English Interpreter In The Polish Army

Let me confess right away that at the time I accepted the assignment of English interpreter in the Polish army, my knowledge of English was poor indeed. Did I say poor? I think it is a gross overstatement of the fact; for how could anyone honestly claim to know the English language, when his whole vocabulary was limited to about seventy words, certainly no more, as mine was then? True, at school I had studied German for four years or so and had also for a short period of time taken some private lessons in Latin. Whatever I still remembered from my school days helped me later with words of Saxon and Latin origin. But my meager vocabulary of English words proper, or what one would call "English" English, had been acquired through my older brother Leon. At home, before the Second World War, he had been in the habit of practicing English with some of his schoolmates. By listening to their conversation, I picked up some words, though I did not always know their correct meaning.

Now, since I have made this confession, you might still be wondering how on earth I agreed to take on such a responsible job. Apart from the army's compulsory assignment and my own desire to leave the former Soviet Union, there were two additional reasons, both indirect and direct. The latter was probably more genuine. The indirect reason was the rivalry between two generals. The more direct reason was the conviction of an army doctor that I could be entrusted with the job. I should explain, perhaps, that the two generals in question were the commanding officers of the Polish Forces in the former Soviet Union and later the Middle East, the late General Anders, and his superior, the late General Sikorski, then commanding the Polish army stationed in Britain under overall British command. It so happened that the Polish Forces in Britain, evacuated from France during the Battle of Dunkirk in 1940, had in their ranks more officers than enlisted men. On the other hand, Polish troops, stationed in the former Soviet Union, had fewer officers but more enlisted men. To rectify the situation, General Anders had been ordered to transfer, from time to time, some of his troops to Britain, to strengthen the forces stationed there. According to rumor, however, he was reluctant (to say the least) to comply with his superior's orders. Apparently, as his opponents claimed, the general strongly believed that whoever commanded the greater number of troops was the real "boss" of the army. The result: Few servicemen left the former Soviet Union for Britain. And those who did leave were not always up to the required standards in terms of health and qualifications.

As for the doctor, he happened to be the same medical officer I first met at a military hospital. It was his unconventional method of treatment and care that had saved my life while I was lying hopelessly ill with typhus. Later on, when I was released from hospital, and by chance transferred to the same camp that he was in, we met again. After a short time, the doctor decided to look after my welfare, assuming the role of a self-appointed guardian. It was from him that I first learned about a new detachment of servicemen being organized and prepared to leave the Soviet Union. He also told me that he had been assigned as a medical officer to accompany the group to Great Britain. What he did not tell me, however, was that the officer in command of this group was looking for someone who could act as English interpreter, and that he had recommended me for the position. A few days later, I was told to report to the officer in charge of our evacuation and transport. A busy man himself, he referred me to one of his assistants, a young lieutenant with a self-important air. After searching through a pile of papers on his desk, he eventually found the document he was looking for. Examining me from head to toe, he again asked me my name and rank, as if to make certain that there was no mistake. Apparently, my low rank and even more, my Jewish name, did not exactly tally with the information on the document. Displaying a distinctly hostile attitude, he scornfully informed me that my nomination as English interpreter had been approved by the army.

Taken aback by this unexpected assignment, I tried to explain to him that my English was hardly sufficient for even a most basic conversation, to say nothing of what is required of an official interpreter. In any case, I said, how could the army have decided on this assignment without even checking if my knowledge of English was good enough for the job? As far as I know, no ordinary soldier was expected to be conversant in any foreign language as part of basic duty requirements. My arguments must have put the young officer off balance, for he angrily retorted that "Jews always try to wriggle out of any assignment," that he did not care whether or not I became an interpreter or even a general. As far as he was concerned, he said, I could take or leave the job and bear the consequences. Anxious to leave the former Soviet Union, I really did not have much of a choice. I resigned myself to the army's decision.

Later on, when I met the doctor, I told him about my new assignment, speculating whether it was with his detachment. Without making any comment, the doctor only gave me a meaningful smile. It was then I realized that my patron must have pulled a few strings to have me included in his group. But when I confided to him my doubts as to whether I would be able to fulfill the requirements of the job, he told me to stop worrying. To set my mind at ease, he also explained that on our way to Britain there would be plenty of time and opportunity for me to master the language. Until then, he said, the little English I already knew would suffice for the immediate needs of the army. So first, under the threat of insubordination in case of refusal, but now reassured and encouraged by the doctor, I decided to take up the challenge. The very first thing I did was to buy myself an introductory English textbook and a Russian-English dictionary. Equipped with these two requisites, I embarked on yet another career in the army.

In the beginning, my activities as interpreter were rather limited. For the most part I had to deal with problems related to military stores, food and medical supplies, living quarters, etc. Sometimes they also included the rather unpleasant task of escorting soldiers to prison or taking them to hospital. Usually, all these activities were carried out through a British army liaison officer. In Iran and Iraq, two countries we had passed in transit from the Soviet Union to Britain, the liaison officer happened to be of Czech origin. As a rule, I conducted all my dealings with him in English. But when stuck, I switched to Polish, trying to make certain that I was fully understood. Although Czech is a Slavic language only remotely like Polish, this alternative and complementary way of communicating with him usually worked well. However, when after a certain time our group left the Iraqi port of Basra aboard the H.M.S. Anglia en route to Bombay, things changed considerably. First of all, the ship we were on carried about 2500 servicemen of various nationalities and religions, forming a truly miniature cosmos. And though limited space and cramped quarters made life somewhat difficult, it also provided all of us with a very interesting and eventful journey. Secondly, the new liaison officer, Captain Young, was of pure British stock, and spoke only English. So, it took me some time to find a satisfactory way of communicating with him, and to settle down to a new working routine aboard the ship.

I experienced my first real test as English interpreter one day when I was told by the liaison officer to go and see Lady Brown. Now, Lady Brown was the wife of a general, the most senior officer in charge of all troops aboard the ship. Puzzled by this rather unusual order, I tried to find out the reason for it, but all the liaison officer was prepared to say was that I should call on her the next day at 9:30 a.m. sharp. The next morning, I walked up to the ship's upper deck, where high-ranking officers were accommodated, and knocked at the door of cabin number seven.

"Come in! Come in!" I heard a pleasant voice calling from inside the cabin. I opened the door and there stood a tall, good-looking woman in her early fifties. Before I had a chance to greet her, she asked: "Are you the Polish contingent's English interpreter?"

"Yes, Madam," I replied, "I am."

"Very good," she said, inviting me to come inside and take a seat opposite her.

Not used to such gentle treatment, I felt rather tense and uncomfortable in the leather-covered easy chair. Lady Brown must have sensed my embarrassment. To put me at my ease, she took out a huge box of chocolates from a drawer. After opening it, she encouraged me to have some. Then, excusing the absence of her husband, who was indisposed that morning, she explained the reason for inviting an English-speaking representative of the Polish detachment.

Lady Brown talked to me for almost an hour or so, rather slowly and in very polished English, trying to make certain that I understood every word she said. At first, she spoke in general terms about music, songs, and folk-dancing. Then she asked me whether we had in our group servicemen who could perform, sing, or play different instruments. Most importantly, however, she wanted to know if there was someone in our group who could take it upon himself to organize and stage a show. Seated opposite Lady Brown, I unexpectedly noticed that under the necklace she wore, there was also a pendant that looked like a Shield of David, the Magen David. Although not quite certain about it, I was overtaken by surprise but quickly regained my composure. Nevertheless, to the end of my visit in Lady Brown's cabin, the intriguing question that kept running through my mind was whether the general's wife was Jewish.

I must confess, though, when leaving her cabin it was more by intuition than through her detailed explanation that I understood what was required of our group. It appeared that we were expected to stage a performance of Polish folk culture, including music, songs, and dancing, for the benefit of other troops aboard the ship. However, what I did not quite make out were important details as to how, when, where, etc., the show was supposed to take place. Strictly speaking, I should have reported immediately to the officer in charge of our group regarding the contents of my conversation with Lady Brown. But since my information was incomplete, and I did not want to reveal that I had missed or had not fully understood what she had said, I decided to postpone the report.

My first thoughts were that, somehow, I had to get hold of the missing details and also find out, by one means or another, whether Lady Brown was Jewish. For some unspecified reason, however, I was not prepared to go back and see Lady Brown again. Trying hard to find an alternative, it dawned on me that perhaps the Greek hairdresser, who worked on the ship, could help me solve the problem. A jovial man, he spoke several languages and most importantly, as befitted a true hairdresser, he was well informed about everything going on aboard the ship. Wasting no time, I went to see the man and explained my problem to him. I also asked him whether Lady Brown was Jewish. He confirmed her Jewish descent adding that, as far as he knew, she came from the well known and highly respected Indian branch of the Sassoon family. As to my main query, however, he told me not to worry unnecessarily, and to come back after 6 o'clock in the evening, It so happened, he said, that Lady Brown had a hairdressing appointment the same day and he was pretty sure he could get all the missing details for me. Sure enough, when I came to see him again just before closing time, he had all the information I needed.

I have chosen to relate the two particular events concerning the Polish army contingent aboard ship because of the distinct manner they had been dealt with by two different nationals. Yet, I cannot refrain from comparing the hostile, almost brutal attitude of the Polish officer towards me because I was Jewish, with that of Lady Brown, who was of Jewish stock, and who acted in such a forbearing and dignified manner, without being aware of my Jewishness.

I experienced another unusual test as English interpreter, while stationed for a short time at a military camp in South Africa. Clairwoods Camp, as it was then called, served as a huge transit base for Allied troops going to and from the Far East. Located near the city of Durban, famous for its coastal beach along the Indian Ocean, it had been designed for the recuperation and recreation of servicemen and other military personnel. But unlike most camps, it provided living quarters and other complementary services of an exceptionally high standard. Judging only by the number of swimming pools, football fields, tennis courts, etc., several canteens, a full-time cinema, as well as a library, it easily compared with the standards and facilities usually found in a five-star hotel, if such a comparison is at all feasible. Stationed temporarily at the camp, together with servicemen of many other nationalities, we waited until a new group would be organized, and transport provided to take us to Britain. And while waiting for a ship to arrive from India, we tried to make the most of the opportunities offered both inside and outside the camp.

One morning, after a few days there, I was told by the officer in charge of our group to see the camp's commandant urgently. As required, I first reported to his adjutant and was told to wait together with others until I'd be summoned to meet the colonel. Looking around, I suddenly realized that I was the only ordinary soldier among many officers, who, like myself, were waiting to see the camp commandant. After twenty minutes or so, my name was called over the loudspeaker, and an orderly ushered me into the office of Colonel McCormick. Answering my salute, the colonel first summed me up from head to toe, and then asked:

"Are you the English interpreter of the Polish contingent?"

"Yes, Sir," I answered, "I am."

"I understand your commanding officer doesn't speak English at all."

"That is correct, Sir," I answered, "he doesn't."

"By the way, what exactly is your rank and name?" he inquired, sizing me up with his penetrating eyes.

"Private, Sir, Pte. Lantner," I repeated.

"Lantner, Lantner, it doesn't sound like a Polish name, or does it?"

"No, Sir, it does not. As a matter of fact, it is a Jewish name."

"Did you say Jewish?"

"Yes, Sir, that is what I said."

"Well, well," muttered the colonel to himself, as though expressing his surprise, or his disapproval, or both. Apparently, it must have been quite a "shocking" experience for an officer of his rank to find himself dealing not only with an ordinary soldier, but one who was a Jew as well. What a disgrace! And all this because the Polish officer in charge of our contingent did not speak English. After a while, when he had regained his composure, he said to me, "It really doesn't matter," and that I could "Just as well sit down." Feeling somewhat uneasy as a result of this unpleasant preliminary conversation with the colonel, I took a seat but at some distance from his desk. Lighting up his pipe and taking a long puff, the colonel continued:

"I am going to read out and explain to you excerpts from an order issued by the British Army's South-Eastern Command. It deals with the Independence Day celebrations of the South African Republic. In a few days," he said, "an order in writing will be sent out to all the officers in camp who are in charge of their respective national contingents. However, since your commanding officer does not speak English, I want to make certain that you understand what it is all about. This will give your group enough time to prepare itself to take part in a military parade and other festivities." Since the colonel was reading out the program with a heavy Scottish accent, it was only with great difficulty that I could follow him and make out the gist of its contents. As for details, I either missed them altogether, or failed to grasp their military significance. Finally, when the colonel finished reading, he asked me if I understood all about the program, and what was required of our contingent. "Of course, Sir," I answered without any hesitation, just to keep up appearances, and not to give myself away.

"Now," said the colonel, "go back to your commanding officer and tell him what I have explained to you."

From my own past experience, I had learned that in such circumstances one must not panic. Stay calm! And so, the very first thing I thought of was to try and get hold of the written order before it reached the officer in charge of our group. Otherwise, I would not be able to translate its detailed contents for him, and my reputation as English interpreter would be at stake. Thinking hard how to overcome this difficulty, it suddenly crossed my mind that the only person who could possibly help me in this situation was Johnny Laird, an Irish infantryman, who served as the colonel's orderly. When approached, he immediately agreed to help, but suggested that he wait until the midday break. His reason was that then he could slip through the half-open office window, and "borrow" the typed order for an hour or so from the colonel. And that is exactly what he did. Once the document was in my hands, I could sit down and with the help of a dictionary and, of course, my friend Johnny, quietly fill in all the missing details. Having translated and pieced together all parts of the order, I was now able to go back and report its full contents to the officer in charge of our group.

The two cases I have described are typical examples of problems I often had to deal with in my capacity as English interpreter. But in actual fact, the number and variety of problems that cropped up during my tenure of this job were far greater, much wider in their scope. Some were serious, others were comic, and still others even tragic, as was the case of a soldier who had died on our way to Britain. He could not be buried properly, since no one knew his religion. The very nature of my job brought me in touch with various military and civilian institutions, such as government offices, local authorities, hospitals, courts, police, prisons, and the like. But it was always people in their various positions that aroused my interest and curiosity. Watching their behavior, attitudes, and decisions, I could easily tell, especially with regard to the military, whether in civilian life the person had been a lawyer, businessman, teacher, or member of any other profession or trade. In short, the job provided many opportunities for observing and studying human behavior in various situations. Characteristically, though, whenever any of those individuals realized that I was Jewish, they would immediately change their conduct, and adopt either a patronizing or a hostile attitude, seldom, if ever, behaving towards me in a normal way.

2 The Misconstrued Communist Slogan: "Those Who Do Not Work Do Not Eat" Or Rather, Are Not Entitled To Any Food

It is well known that the object of propaganda is to disseminate information containing facts, arguments, rumors, half-truths, and also frequently lies – all to influence public opinion. Such one-sided presentation helps spread the ideology of a party, movement, or regime in a given country. Although the use of propaganda activity as such is not new, the term itself is comparatively modern. It derives its name from the Latin: *Congregatio de Propaganda Fide*, the Congregation for the Propagation of the Faith, an organization set up by the Roman Catholic Church in 1622, to carry out missionary work.

The more modern concept of propaganda, especially one with political objectives, was introduced in the 20th century. Responsible for this innovation were principally two leading totalitarian states, namely: the Soviet Union and Nazi Germany. The regimes in both countries imposed strict control over all information disseminated; forcing the mass media to uphold the government's power and authority, in order to spread its political aspirations and objectives. To manipulate the people's beliefs and attitudes, they also employed a variety of additional means and methods. Among them, a particularly significant part was played by organized rallies, processions, marches, and parades. Tens of thousands and more (uniformed in Germany) party members and their supporters, carrying flags, banners, posters, and other propaganda emblems, participated in those mass displays, demonstrating their political and numerical strength. However, the main instruments of the regimes' propaganda, apart from the written media, were radio and films, reaching wide audiences, both inside and outside the borders of their respective countries.

In this connection, it is also especially important to underline those states' effective use of various propaganda slogans, short and well-thought-out phrases, employed to foster their political objectives. Unlike commercial jingles, designed to advertise and promote the sale of various products and services, the purpose of their short propaganda messages was to appeal to mass audiences, so as to make people behave or act in a certain manner. The catchier the phrase, the easier it was remembered and, therefore, more likely to produce the desired results.

As far as anti-Semitic slogans are concerned, however, it is important to distinguish between their varying natures and the different purposes they are designed to fulfill.

The "reasonable" slogan is one which purports to have a motive or justification for a certain specific cause or action. And so, for instance, two of the most widely propagated and officially sanctioned anti-Semitic slogans in Poland, between the two World Wars, were: "POLSKA DLA POLAKOW!", i.e., "Poland for Poles!", and "ZYDZI DO PALESTYNY!", meaning "Jews to Palestine!" These slogans caught on, despite the fact that the Jews of Poland had contributed greatly to the development and well-being of the country for a thousand years. The anti-Jewish cleansing policy, pursued by successive Polish governments during the interwar period, but especially after World War II, resulted in an *en masse* exodus of Polish Jews, who lost all desire to return and live there again. The result is that there are practially no Jews left in Poland today.

The emotional slogan, on the other hand, is one which easily arouses people's feelings to the point of becoming inflammatory and often calls for direct action. One such slogan, widely circulated in Czarist Russia, was "BEIY ZYDOV, SPASAIY ROSSIYU." It means "Strike the Jews down and save Russia!" Another slogan, perhaps somewhat less inflammatory but, nevertheless, with a similarly strong anti-Jewish message, was used in the Soviet Union. "TZIONISTY ETO WRAGIY NARODA!" – "Zionists are the enemies of the People!" In this slogan, the word "Zionists" is used instead of "Jews," because anti-Semitism was officially prohibited after the revolution. Unofficially, however, not only was it widely practiced by ordinary people, but also by the Soviet authorities themselves, who often initiated and were responsible for many anti-Jewish activities. Suffice to mention the notorious "Doctor's Plot" during Stalin's regime, the mass dismissal of Jews from their jobs, the execution of Jewish intellectuals in 1956 on Stalin's direct orders, the show trials and execution of Jews initiated by Khrushchev for so-called "economic crimes," and outbursts of popular anti-Semitism during the Kosygin and Brezhnev period.

The deceptive slogan is one that purports to give a positive idea or impression but, in truth, is false and intentionally misleading. Among many of the anti-Semitic slogans devised and used by Nazi propaganda organs during World War II was one particularly perfidious in its treachery. I refer, of course, to the motto: "ARBEIT MACHT FREI," or "Work liberates," which appeared over the entrances to all Nazi concentration camps. This notorious phrase turned out to be an exceptionally wicked deceit, for all those so-called "work camps," erected by the Germans, had been places of torture and extermination. In these camps many millions of innocent people, the majority of whom were Jews, met their deaths in the most brutal manner, murdered by the Nazis and their henchmen.

Having surveyed the propaganda role of various political phrases, let me now tell you in some detail a story about the repercussions of one such notorious and widely circulated slogan. Coined by the Soviet propaganda machine during World War II, it appeared to carry a perfectly positive message but which, in effect turned out to be a deceitful sham. As such, it misled and detrimentally affected tens of millions of people, among them also a great proportion of the Jewish population that lived under the Soviet regime.

My story goes back to the early forties when, fleeing from the advancing German army with David, a friend of mine, I eventually reached the city of Tashkent, capital of Uzbekistan in central Asia. After spending a few days exploring the possibilities of settling in the city, David and I came to the conclusion that our chances of doing so were practically nil. First of all, Tashkent was almost saturated with evacuees and refugees who had arrived earlier from Belorussia, the Ukraine, Russia, and other Soviet republics. Secondly, while some select and specialized jobs were still available, accommodation in the city itself was not. This meant that anyone taking a job here would have to live outside Tashkent, and travel into the city every day. And since the pay offered was comparatively low and the cost of living high, the whole proposition was not worth considering. So we decided that our chances of settling down might be better in some smaller place. Before deciding on any specific locality, however, we were anxious to obtain information about possibilities in other towns and cities. Unfortunately, neither government nor municipal authorities provided such an information service for the convenience of refugees.

At this point, my friend David suggested that we go to the local bazaar and meet up with other refugees, who might possibly be more informed than we were. He was right. It turned out that during the war, as in the Middle Ages, the bazaar had become an important institution throughout Soviet Central Asia. For here the paths of people from various walks of life crossed. People would come to barter certain goods for others. Money was rarely used. Here, too, people would exchange information, from the current situation at the front to the latest local gossip. Refugees often struck up new acquaintanceships and friendships here. Thus, the next morning at the bazaar, we met a couple of refugees who, for reasons similar to ours, contemplated leaving Tashkent for Namangan. Having heard of greater possibilities in that city, from other people as well we decided to join them and travel together.

The city of Namangan, the administrative center of the region, oblast, as it is called in Russian, turned out to be a bustling, medium-sized industrial city of the Uzbek Republic. Situated in the northern Fergana Valley, it had become the business center of the most fertile cotton-growing region in the country. In the Middle Ages, an important caravan route from India to China passed through Namangan and a sister city, Kokand. By the mid-eighteenth century, its many craftsmen had made it one of the foremost cities in the entire area. Also, in the same century, Namangan had become part of the khanate of Kokand, and the center of a political unit. Industrial processing of local agricultural raw materials, particularly cotton, began to develop after the Fergana Valley was annexed by Russia in 1876. In more recent times the city, as well as the whole region, had become known throughout the former Soviet Union for its highly developed cotton industry.

To our great surprise, as soon as we arrived at the Namangan railway station, we were met by several representatives of both local industry and communal settlements, or *kolkhozy*, as they are called in Russian. Each of them was offering a job to almost every refugee who was prepared to sign up. In fact, the competition between the various representatives was so strong that they tried to outbid one another by offering higher pay, better conditions, or both.

As we discovered later, the reason for this unusual competition was a general call-up by the Soviet army that had left many plants, factories, and other industrial and agricultural units with a greatly depleted work force. As is well known, in a centrally controlled economy, annual targets for each economic unit are expected not only to be fulfilled, but to be exceeded. Any failure to reach the set target, for whatever reason, would reflect on the unit's poor management. In some cases, this would lead to punitive repercussions. The fulfillment of production targets in wartime became even more demanding than during peace. No wonder, then, that all prospective employers, or rather their representatives, were anxious to fill all their vacant positions as quickly as possible, even with untrained people, whose physical, though not mental capacity was greatly reduced. In such a favorable situation, with workers very much in demand, David and I decided not to hurry but explore some additional work possibilities, though not through intermediaries. Since it was already getting dark, we had to find lodgings for the night. Someone suggested the nearby tea house, where, for a nominal fee, one could spend the night. Having already slept in so many odd places during our long wanderings, we decided to try an Uzbek tea house as yet another change.

The nearest equivalent to an Asian tea house or *tchaichana*, as it is called in Uzbek, would be the European café, and that only insofar as its social functions are concerned. In all other respects, there is no similarity between them whatsoever. First of all, the *tchaichana* is exclusively frequented by men. They go there to meet their male acquaintances and friends for casual talk and a game of chess or dice. Then, apart from hot, strong, and bitter green tea and cool spring water, nothing else is served there. Sitting cross-legged on a carpeted floor and leaning against cushions while socializing, the men drink enormous quantities of tea, emptying one cup after another.

Uzbek people consider that their tea, unlike ours, possesses healing properties. But while I myself could not verify their claim, this soothing drink proved to be a very effective means of quenching one's thirst, especially on a hot and dry summer day. Usually, this social activity in a *tchaichana* goes on till the late evening hours. Before closing time, the men gradually begin to disperse, heading for their homes. But those who have paid the required fee stay on, preparing themselves to spend the night there on a thinly carpeted floor with no bedding.

Just as we were getting ready to stretch out on the floor, one of our neighbors warned us to beware of thieves. The night before, he said, there had been a few thefts, but the victims were advised not to complain, for fear of repercussions. Since we had no valuables and hardly any belongings, we paid little attention to his warning. But when I woke up the next morning, in place of my almost brand new leather shoes, I had on my feet a pair of old and torn galoshes, despite the fact that when lying down, as advised, I did not take off my shoes at all. How on earth the thief managed to exchange his old galoshes for my practically new shoes was a mystery I could not understand. And when I went to see the owner of the place to complain about the theft, he measured me up from head to toe, and with an ironical smile on his face replied, "You should be satisfied with the pair of galoshes he left you with. Otherwise you would have to walk about barefoot." Having learned my lesson, I swore then and there not to sleep at an Uzbek tea house any more.

On the advice of some local people, David and I went to the city's regional government agency for textile industries to find out about job opportunities. We were told that the local cotton industry, especially their mills, offered higher pay and better working conditions than other industries in the area. After an interview of only ten minutes or so at their personnel department, we were hired and sent to work at No. 5 State Cotton Mill. There, the mill's head foreman explained to me and another refugee worker the requirements of our jobs. Together with two other workers in the team, we were to feed raw cotton to a conveyor belt, which carried it to a milling press. Because of his previous experience, David was given a job as a wages clerk in the mill's accounting department. The three of us were told to start work the next day, and in the meantime to go back and complete all the necessary paperwork at the agency.

During the first week on the job I was engrossed in learning the ropes of my trade. After a month or so, I became fairly well familiarized with all the mill's production stages, so much so that after a short time I was often asked to fill the place of any missing worker on the production line. Transferred to the mill's engine room on the work manager's recommendation, I worked there first as assistant to the shift operator and then as an independent operator. Though my status and pay were now appreciably higher, I had great doubts as to whether I should have agreed to accept the position. One reason was that my technical knowledge, at the time, was not sufficient for filling the job of an independent operator. The other reason was that, though an inexperienced youth, I was made to shoulder the heavy burden of operating the mill's engine room during an eight-hour shift. The truth is that, from the very beginning, I did not want to take on the job at all. But because of pressure exerted by the works manager, and his promise of help in case of need, I was talked into accepting the position.

Strictly speaking, there were only two alternatives before me. Either I accepted the offered job, or I refused, and thereby exposed myself to the possibility of being dismissed for insubordination. And dismissal from a job, especially in wartime, meant suffering from various mistreatments, including a cut of the daily bread ration by half, dismissal from the hostel, and, worst of all, exclusion from getting any other job. In this connection, I should explain that in the Soviet Union, every person starting his or her first job was issued with a personal worker's logbook, *trudovaiya knizka*, as it is called in Russian. In it, every successive employer would periodically enter all relevant information regarding the person's performance, throughout the years of his or her employment. Reasons for dismissal, transfer, or leaving one's job, were automatically entered in the logbook. It was on the basis of this information that a person could be accepted or rejected when trying to get a new job. It goes without saying that under such a strict system of workers' control, one's freedom to change his or her job, for whatever reason, was rather limited, if it existed at all.

During my first few weeks on the new job, the mill was running more or less without any serious trouble. Then one day, when I was working on the morning shift, a fire suddenly broke out in the engine room, bringing the whole mill to a standstill. As a result, I was suspended from work, though not dismissed.

The management blamed me for the fire, but could not agree on the charge to be brought against me. The chief engineer maintained that the fire was the result of a deliberate act of sabotage. But the works manager was prepared to settle for a lesser charge, namely, that of gross negligence on my part. A short investigation by representatives of the works committee disclosed, however, that the fire was due not to any fault of mine, but to excessive frictional heat, caused by overloading the mill's cotton press. In simple language, this meant that its Uzbek crew, anxious to earn a higher premium in addition to their basic wage, had operated the press above its permitted capacity.

Furthermore, I myself discovered that it was common practice to go beyond the permitted working capacity at any bench or process work-station throughout the mill. Apparently, all this was done with the knowledge and tacit agreement of the mill's Uzbek lower and middle staff, in opposition to the expressed policy of its management, who were predominantly of Russian nationality. On the face of it, the policy issue centered on the problem of improving the cotton's quality, but not at the expense of the quantities produced. In actual fact, the aim was to prevent the Uzbek personnel from running the mill for their own narrow financial benefit, at the expense of the war effort and its requirements.

To complicate matters further, the mill's newly appointed director happened to be of Jewish stock. He had been sent from Moscow to relieve a local man, accused of sabotaging the war effort. However, the mill's chief engineer, who was an Uzbek nationalist and a self-declared anti-Semite, tried hard not only to discredit the new manager, but also to get rid of all Jewish refugees working at the mill. In this way, without my having any say in the matter, my case now became another subject of dispute among the parties concerned. It also brought to the surface the long-standing animosity between management and the Russian secretary of the works committee. The fact that the three parties concerned differed on how the mill should be run, though not directly connected with my case, added a Jewish aspect as well.

Suspended from work with no pay and placed on a reduced bread ration, I had to find a way of earning a living until my case was resolved. Without my work logbook – retained at the mill – I could not be employed in any other workplace regularly. The only occupation I could possibly engage in was work as a self-employed artisan or craftsman. But since I had no training in either of these occupations, the possibilities of finding work were limited indeed. About this time, I became friendly with a young Russian evacuee, also a resident of our hostel, called Leonid. He, too, was suspended from his job, but for being a chronic absentee. As we shared the same fate and were suffering from hunger, he proposed one day that we stop idling and start *organizing* food for ourselves. By *organizing*, I should explain, he meant stealing from farmers, who were bringing their produce to be sold or exchanged at the local bazaar. Hesitating at first, but really not having much of a choice, I agreed to his proposal, and he initiated me into the secrets of the *trade*.

My new job would be to choose a suitable stallholder at the bazaar, engage him in conversation, and offer to exchange a pair of shoes or a shirt for some of his produce. While the man focused his attention on examining the item, Leonid, running past us, would grab some of the produce from the stall and disappear in the crowd. To ensure success, we had to comply with two basic requirements. First, the chosen stallholder should not be a young man, so his reaction would be comparatively slow. Next, the operation must take place at the height of the bazaar's activity, when crowds were thickest and, therefore, Leonid's escape safest. For some time the system worked fairly well, until one day Leonid was caught in the act of stealing. But since the militiaman happened to be Russian, like Leonid, and the stallholder Uzbek, Leonid managed to wriggle out of it simply by declaring that he was hungry. After some time, I suggested to Leonid that, instead of stealing food at the bazaar, we could earn it by helping the farmers unload their produce and carry it to their stalls. But since Leonid had a natural aversion to work, any kind of work, I decided to dissolve the *partnership*, though not our friendship.

Left on my own, I now became a manual laborer, working at the bazaar and doing various odd jobs, mostly helping farmers carry their produce. Twice a day, early in the morning and late in the evening, just before closing time, I would go to the bazaar to carry out my chores. For the work I did, instead of money I was paid in kind, that is to say, given vegetables and fruits, but no bread. To some extent, this arrangement suited me fine, for between the morning and evening chores I could go to the public library and spend my free time reading and studying. In addition, every so often I would call on Comrade Anna Ivanova, secretary of the mill's works committee, to find out if there was any progress, or even a decision made in my case. She would usually receive me in a friendly manner over a glass of strong Russian tea, and inquire about my well-being.

Regarding my case, however, she was convinced that in the end management would accept my innocence, and I would be reinstated in my job. In the meantime, she advised me to be patient, and continue with my studies.

On my next visit to Comrade Ivanova, she was exceptionally friendly. But instead of discussing my case, out of the blue she proposed that I take part in the staging of Anton Chekhov's play "Uncle Vanya" by the mill's theatrical group. At first, I was taken aback by her unexpected proposal, and as an excuse claimed to have no acting ability. In any case, I said, my Russian was not good enough for me to appear on stage. But Comrade Ivanova insisted, and would not take no for an answer. Moreover, she volunteered to work with me on improving my Russian pronunciation. Confronted by her insistence, but also anxious to retain her positive attitude towards me, I reluctantly agreed to participate in the play. Three times a week, we rehearsed our parts with Anna Ivanova, who, apart from directing the play, also watched over my pronunciation and diction.

Despite frequent rehearsals, we seemed to be making little progress, partly because some members of the group were called up for service in the Soviet army, and others had to take their places in the three-shift running of the mill. We had advanced so little, in fact, that after some time I came to the inescapable conclusion that the whole thing was one big deception. Continuing rehearsals was not so much the result of a desire to stage the play as an excuse for providing those in the group with free meals and supplementary bread rations.

It is a well-known fact that in the Soviet Union people engaged in the arts, especially those working for or connected with keeping up the people's morale, benefited from certain privileges, free meals and supplementary bread rations among them. And so, the famous communist slogan, "Those Who Do Not Work Do Not Eat," became an empty phrase, for, paradoxically, as it turned out in my case, almost half of the participants in the drama group never worked at all. Nevertheless, they received the extra food denied to those who did work. Soon, however, this theatrical enterprise, artificially maintained by Comrade Ivanova, had to be disbanded. And so, as a result of it, all its participants, including myself, forfeited the privileges enjoyed hitherto.

The slogan, "Those Who Do Not Work Do Not Eat," or rather are not entitled to any food, coined by Soviet propaganda during World War II, though not specifically aimed at the Jews, affected them more than any other ethnic group in the country. To perceive the reason for it, it is important to emphasize the fact that, as a result of social changes that followed the October Revolution in 1917, the majority of Jews in the Soviet Union found themselves in the middle levels of the country's society. As such, they and others in that group were considered by the communist regime to be the least productive element of the Soviet population, as far as their contribution to the war effort was concerned. As a result, they suffered from shortages of food, especially from a very limited allocation of the daily bread ration, then the staple diet in the country. On the other hand, peasants, artisans, craftsmen and the like, directly involved in the production and supply of much needed food and other goods, were regarded by the Soviet regime to be the productive elements of society. As such, they enjoyed increased allocations of food, including the daily bread ration, and were entitled to various other limited benefits.

This classification, or rather division, into more and less productive elements of society in wartime could, perhaps, be justified, had it not been for the fact that a fair percentage of the country's citizens, who belonged to the establishment, or *nomenklatura*, as they are called in Russian, enjoyed both officially sanctioned privileges, and additional benefits denied to those outside their circle. Among the roughly 300 million people who comprised the Soviet Union, the number of privileged citizens, when multiplied by members of their families, friends, and close associates, added up to several tens of millions. No wonder then, that as a result, ordinary citizens of the country chronically suffered from shortages of food and other basic commodities. In such circumstances, the gap between the privileged and the underprivileged citizens of the Soviet Union constantly widened, splitting society into rich and poor, more particularly into "haves and have nots." And all this in striking contradiction to the officially held *holy* principle of a fair distribution of goods in their socialist and *just* society.

3 From The Humiliation Of Wearing The Yellow Badge To Conducting Hymn Music At Church Services

Among the many anti-Jewish laws enacted by the Church during the Middle Ages there was one in particular which defined the status of Jews as inferior to that of Christians. Based on the Augustan doctrine that Jews are slaves, it required that they should be kept in perpetual servitude for the crimes committed against Christianity. Consequently, Jews were forbidden to hold any position of authority or to mix with Christians in the various lands of their abode. The aim of this abusive legislation, as defined by the Lateran Council of 1215 was "to protect Christians from all the wicked influences that Jews exert on Christian Society." And so, to segregate and distinguish Jews from Christians, Jews were required to wear distinctive clothing, including a conical hat and a yellow badge. This compulsory differentiation between Jew and non-Jew was intended to make the Jew easily recognizable and, therefore, exposed to unprovoked abuse and attack. It is important to stress the fact that the yellow badge, or Badge of Shame as it was called, had been in use for centuries in most Christian lands, though with various degrees of enforcement, until the French Revolution in 1789.

In 1941, during the Second World War, the yellow badge was again officially introduced by the Germans in several countries under their occupation. All Jews, regardless of age or sex, were compelled to wear the yellow Star of David. By introducing this distinctive sign, the Germans aimed to create a barrier between Jews and non-Jews, so as to restrict the movements of Jews. To a large extent, the Germans achieved this aim, despite the opposition they encountered in certain occupied countries, rendering enforcement of the order somewhat difficult.

It is also important here to stress the fact that, before the Germans established Jewish ghettos in their occupied territories, Jews increasingly tended to gather in particular districts, for fear of being arrested and deported to concentration camps. The result was that a Jew could either conceal the special sign, thus becoming an offender liable to be deported to a concentration camp, or wear the badge and become easy prey to enemies. There is no doubt that the yellow badge was an effective means for the Germans to facilitate their plan to exterminate the Jews.

There were also other medieval canon law restrictions, intended to humiliate the Jews publicly. For instance, laws forbade the Jews to work on Sundays, walk in the streets on Christian holidays, and enter church premises. Paradoxically, it was a Polish army Catholic colonel who, some fifty years ago, disregarded this last canonical restriction, long before the official and radical change of attitude towards the Jews by the

Second Vatican Council in October 1965. He did so by ordering a Jewish military bandleader and his Jewish musicians not only to enter church premises, but to play hymn music each Sunday, while Mass was celebrated by a Catholic chaplain. For the background and conditions that had led up to this extraordinary development, it is necessary to take you right back to the very beginning of this unusual story and relate it in greater detail.

In 1942, reports from the war fronts were gloomy for the Allies. In Europe, the Germans had broken the defense lines of the river Volga, threatening the city of Stalingrad. In Africa, Rommel's army had reached the approaches of the Nile, endangering Egypt and other neighboring countries. But here, in the city of Namangan, the industrial center of the Soviet Republic of Uzbekistan, there was no immediate danger of any hostile military operations. Apart from the usual shortage of food, clothing, and other essential commodities, people went about their daily lives following a normal pattern. As for myself, at the time, I was working as a porter at the local railroad station. Late one evening, while getting ready to go on the night shift, I noticed among the many passengers who had arrived a military man wearing a uniform I had never seen before. At first, I thought he was an officer in the service of some foreign country. But when I approached the man, I discovered, to my great astonishment, that his insignia, though not his uniform, were those of a Polish officer. He must have noticed my confusion, for without being approached, he turned to me and said: "Yes, yes, you are not mistaken; I am an officer of the newly formed Polish army."

Bewildered by this young officer's sudden appearance, I asked him how it was that in this part of the Soviet Union we had not heard about this newly formed Polish army. His answer was that for precisely this reason he had been sent by his superiors to make arrangements for the registration and selection of suitable former Polish citizens eager to join the resurrected army. This, he said, would be done with the assistance and cooperation of the local Soviet military authorities. Only after registration and a preliminary selection by them, he explained, would the candidates appear before a Polish military induction board.

He also told me that the formation of the Polish army had come about as the result of an agreement between the Polish government-in-exile, at the time based in Britain, and the Soviet Union. Its detailed terms had been specified in the so-called Sikorski-Maisky Agreement of July 30, 1941. It was this agreement also that ensured the release of all Polish officers and soldiers, as well as hundreds of thousands of Polish civilians from Soviet prisons, camps, deportation and penal settlements. Despite undernourishment and physical weakness, the Polish military authorities expected that there would be enough suitable candidates amongst them to draft into the army. Before we parted, the young officer also told me to watch out for a draft notice that should appear in the next day or two in the daily press sponsored by the Soviet government.

Every morning for about a week, I impatiently searched for this draft notice in the official press but, unfortunately, could not find any trace of it. However, two weeks later, by chance passing the Soviet local *voyenkomat*, the military registration and enlistment office, I spotted one single draft notice obscurely posted on a side wall. The reason for this rather "modest" and half-hidden notification, as I later learned, was that the Soviet government, after signing the aforementioned agreement, had some misgivings. Therefore, for reasons of its own, the government was not too anxious that great numbers of Polish citizens join this newly established army. Nevertheless, two days later I decided to register with the Polish military mission in Namangan. After filling in a form with all relevant personal data, and a short interview, I was told to go home and wait for a reply. And indeed, exactly ten days later, I received a summons to appear before the Polish induction board. Once in possession of the summons, I hurried to say goodbye to my Russian friend Leonid. On hearing that I was leaving Namangan to join the army, he burst into tears and, after kissing me on both cheeks, wished me the best of luck. Though somewhat embarrassed, I accepted this typical Russian way of parting from a male friend.

Early the next morning, I arrived by train at a small Uzbek township called Kermine. Travelling with me were a number of compatriots who, like myself, were eager to join the army. After walking from the station for an hour or so, we arrived at the army's Seventh Division headquarters. Located in a number of small one-story houses in the middle of a vast and barren field, it looked more like an abandoned farm than a military establishment. I had no difficulty in finding the induction building, as it was surrounded by a huge crowd of angry men trying desperately to get inside. Some, who had probably arrived two or three days earlier, were now standing in line and waiting their turn to enter. But others, newcomers like myself, had no choice but to sit or lie down on the ground and patiently await their turn.

Since no shelter had been provided, we were forced to sleep under the open sky. To protect ourselves from freezing, we kept fires burning throughout the nights. During the day, we just lay or sat there passing the time by playing cards, chatting, and exchanging our prison and labor camp experiences. In short, a sorry and pitiful sight of untidy, sick, and impatient men, sleeping, eating, and relieving themselves in one huge open field. The lucky ones, who eventually managed to get inducted, left for their units, making room for newcomers to take their places.

Others, however, were less lucky even before they went through the drafting process. I refer to Polish citizens of various ethnic groups such as Ukrainians, Belorussians, and Jews. There were two reasons for this selective induction. One, a semi-legal one, was connected with the annexation of eastern Poland by the Soviets in October 1939. As far as the semi-legal reason was concerned, the Soviet authorities had at first made no distinction between the various ethnic groups of Polish citizens joining their army. But after some time they decided to claim the former inhabitants of these territories as their own citizens, thus barring their recruitment into the Polish army. Apparently, by doing so the Soviets wanted to renew and secure their claim to the eastern part of Poland, annexed under the Ribbentrop-Molotov agreement of June 1939. The other reason was the Polish authorities' extreme bias and prejudice against their own ethnic citizens. This was based on, and connected with, the political, economic, and religious history of pre-war Poland.

It is important to stress here that before the war, the eastern part of Poland had been mainly settled by Ukrainians and Belorussians. Both ethnic groups objected very much to Polish minority domination, and developed very strong national movements, so much so that during the period between the two world wars, their resistance to Polish rule often led to acts of terrorism and repression. But now, with the objective of preventing any future Soviet territorial claims, the army, acting on instructions from the Polish government-in-exile, adopted a middle course. It inducted Ukrainian and Belorussian nationals, but on a very selective basis and in limited numbers.

With regard to Poland's Jewish citizens, the reason for their limited induction into the army was altogether different. Here anti-Semitism, widespread among Poles, played an important part. Originally based on religious premises, it had spread and penetrated into political and economic spheres as well, especially after the First World War. But by comparison with the other two ethnic groups, the Jewish population boasted a proportionally greater number of professional people. It so happened that the newly formed Polish army could not fill some of its specialized and technical posts for lack of sufficient numbers of professionals. And so, out of sheer necessity more than anything else, the army drafted a limited number of Jewish citizens. Among them were professionals such as doctors, dentists, engineers, radio technicians, musicians, and the like. But as usually happens in such circumstances, paradoxes could not be avoided, as the following story will show.

Lying on the ground near the induction building, I was talking to some of the men who had arrived at the place a few days earlier. While talking, we were also watching those standing in line waiting their turn to enter. Suddenly one of the doors opened wide and a uniformed man came out of the building. He pushed his way through the surrounding crowd and then, going from one group of men to another, inquired if there were any musicians present. When he came near our group and spoke to one of the men, his deep baritone voice somehow sounded familiar to me. But it was only when I saw his face that I immediately recognized him. And when, in turn, he approached me and asked if by any chance I played some musical instrument, I replied in the negative. But I also told him that not so very long ago I had danced to the music of his band. Utterly surprised, he asked me if I knew who he was. "Certainly," I replied. "When we met the very first time you were the band leader of the well-known dance music orchestra bearing your own name." He was visibly moved by the fact that here was someone who remembered him and his famous band from the good old pre-war times. He then expressed his regret that I did not play any musical instrument. Otherwise, he said, there would have been no difficulty getting me enlisted to join the Polish army military band, of which he was now the bandmaster.

Later on, when I asked the man, now a sergeant major, how he himself had managed to join the army, he told me the following story. In June 1939, he and members of his band, together with their families, had gone on a concert tour to eastern Poland. Just as they were to return home, war broke out, and they could not get back to their native Warsaw. Forced to stay on, but now under the Soviet regime, the band continued touring the cities and towns of the occupied territory, playing to their devoted audiences. But three months or so later, after an unsuccessful attempt at illegally crossing the newly established Soviet-German border, they were caught and deported to Siberia. Released in October 1941, they left Siberia and made their way to Uzbekistan. Here, at Kermine, together with other Polish ex-prisoners, they had come to join the newly formed army. And in spite of the fact that they were all Jewish, their chances of getting accepted were fairly good. Nevertheless, they also encountered some difficulties. At first, the army board agreed to induct only some of the band's musicians. But since he laid down the condition, as band leader, that either all of them were accepted or none would individually join the army, the board had no choice but to agree. Then another problem cropped up, namely the question of army support for the families of those musicians who were married. Again the board objected, but after prolonged negotiations, it finally agreed. And that was how this man and his musicians managed to be drafted into the Polish army.

This is not the end of the story – it has an epilogue. According to the sergeant major, the changeover from dance to military music was not so difficult. As experienced musicians, the band members set to meet their new challenge with vigor and seriousness. And they were able to do so, especially after they had been equipped with a complete set of brand new musical instruments, donated by Poles from the United States. In addition, they also received several dozen musical scores especially written for military bands. On the other hand, band members initially did have some difficulties readjusting to the requirements of a military regime. But after a comparatively short time, with a number of additional musicians and a lot of practice, they formed a proper military band, able to play at all occasions, whenever called upon. Then one day the sergeant major was told by his immediate superior to report to Colonel J., in charge of the army's education and religious matters.

As ordered, early the very next day, he reported to the army's divisional headquarters. The colonel, a university professor in civilian life, received the sergeant major in a friendly manner. After offering him a seat, the colonel expressed his satisfaction with the progress made by the band under the sergeant-major's direction. Then, somewhat hesitantly, the colonel also told him about the new demand imposed on the band. It had come from the divisional commander himself, he explained, ordering their participation at Sunday church services.

The colonel also told the sergeant major that he had already ordered the appropriate musical scores from London, and expected to receive them within about eight weeks. On hearing of this new demand, the sergeant major replied that, as far as he and other Jewish members of the band were concerned, there was no problem whatsoever. After all, he said, when ordered, they would be going to church to play and not to pray. As to the printed music ordered from London, he suggested saving precious waiting time. When asked by the colonel how he proposed to do away with the required musical scores, he replied that the problem could be easily solved: If the divisional chaplain could hum the various hymns sung when celebrating mass, he, the sergeant major, could write them down and then prepare musical scores for the whole band. On hearing the proposed solution, the colonel praised the sergeant major for his suggestion, adding that, in spite of the prevailing negative attitude towards the Jews, he himself "had always regarded the Jews as intelligent and capable people."

* * *

And that is the story of how the once well-known dance music composer and orchestra leader, the son of a poor Jewish *klezmer*, a village musician, turned into a successful military bandmaster in the Polish army. In spite of the fact that in the past Jews had been strictly forbidden by canon law even so much as to enter church premises, now the sergeant major and his Jewish musicians were not only allowed, but actually ordered to do so. In his new capacity as a military bandmaster, in addition to conducting the band at church services, he was writing down and preparing all the required hymn music. What an ironical paradox, this requirement that Jews fulfill a function in direct contravention to the previously enacted humiliating and abusive anti-Jewish canon of Church law!

4 Who Exactly Is Running The Black Market And Why, Especially In A State Controlled Economy

Among many of the unjust and baseless accusations widely circulated in Christian countries is one which claims that Jews are responsible for creating and running the black market. Now, the very first thing to realize about the black market is that it is not a deliberate creation of any people, but an indirect result of a country's controlled economy. Any economy that is planned, instituted and supervised by a government imposes certain restrictions and limitations, different from those of a market economy. With the principle of full employment under such a system, there is bound to be a certain disparity between people's earnings and their expenditure. And so to close this gap, at least partially, a government with such an economy is forced to subsidize certain foodstuffs and other basic commodities.

However, since these subsidies are usually not sufficient, the majority of ordinary people have no choice but to seek some additional sources of income, either by extra work or some other, often illegal, activity. Without free and unrestricted interplay between the market forces of supply and demand, and in spite of partial subsidies by a government operating such a system, ordinary people continue to suffer shortages of foodstuffs and other commodities. In such circumstances the black market, though by itself not a welcome phenomenon, nevertheless fulfills an important function. It serves as an alternative source for supplementing the very goods and services a government cannot provide for its citizens. So, instead of having one overall economy as in a free market, under a centrally controlled system, there are two parallel channels of economic activity enabling sellers and buyers to operate, though not officially, side by side, complementing each other.

It is necessary to stress the fact that, in any country with an economy controlled by the government, every second or third person, whatever his race, nationality, or religion, is compelled to engage in some form of black-market operations in order to survive. This is done either directly by selling goods and services at inflated prices, or indirectly, by exchanging them for other goods and services at their respective values. To illustrate how a black market operates, here is a typical example: Suppose that a government mill is supplied with 100 tons of corn to be milled. According to the set standard, the mill is expected to produce 94 tons of pure flour. The six ton difference is comprised of two tons of permissible wastage, and another four tons of bran left over from the process.

However, by reducing the wastage quantity by half, the mill is able to produce an additional ton of corn flour. This extra flour is then divided between the mill's management and its workers, and eventually finds its way on the black market. A more ingenious and refined way of producing extra flour above the set standard is by exposing it for a short period of time to steam or some other form of moisture. After such treatment its weight is increased, and all the extra flour is then sold on the black market. By the way, this method of treatment by moisture is also successfully applied to such commodities as sugar, salt, coffee, tea, and any other product that absorbs moisture and is sold by weight. In fact, there are practically no limits to people's ingenuity and inventiveness in finding new ways and means of circumventing any rules and regulations imposed by a government-controlled economy.

It may also be of interest to note that at one time it was estimated that over 60 percent of the Soviet Union's total turnover of consumer goods was processed through the black market. For other goods, officially carried by special government shops that dealt exclusively in hard currencies, the estimated percentage was even higher. It has been and still is an established fact that many goods originally acquired from government and cooperative shops eventually find their way on the black market. But there, paradoxically, they are subjected to market forces of supply and demand, but always at inflated prices. Here, then, is a typical story, one of many black market encounters I experienced myself while in the Soviet Union.

Apart from the proverbial shortages of food and clothing in the Soviet Union, there was yet another serious problem that cropped up during World War II. What I have in mind is the extreme difficulties encountered by the population in maintaining personal and general cleanliness. The chronic scarcity and often total lack of cleansing materials, especially of ordinary soap, on the official market made it difficult, if not impossible, to maintain a minimal standard of personal hygiene. Even if a small percentage of the population managed, from time to time, to get hold of a limited quantity of soap at black market prices, there was still the need to find a solution for dealing with dirty underwear and outer clothing that had to be washed every so often. The same applied to living quarters, community and other public buildings, where floors, walls, doors and windows had to be kept clean. Water, even hot water, could not do the trick without some detergent and other cleansing materials.

In this respect, especially lamentable was the position of many millions of evacuees and refugees. Forced by war to move from one area or region to another, and often to live in groups and cramped conditions in such public places as parks, schoolyards, air raid shelters and the like, they had scarcely any opportunity and means to wash. No wonder, then, that in a very short time epidemics broke out, affecting a great number of people throughout the country. The most widespread of them all was typhus, but dysentery and tuberculosis claimed a fair share of the lives, too. The main culprits responsible for transmitting the typhus disease were body lice. Without proper sanitary measures, they thrived and rapidly multiplied undisturbed. Other contributing factors to the spread of epidemics were malnutrition, vitamin deficiency, and physical weakness of the human body.

To prevent falling victim to any of these diseases, I followed a number of precautionary measures. Apart from observing as strict personal cleanliness of both body and clothing as was possible, I also avoided overcrowded and stuffy public places as much as I could. When two fatal cases of typhus occurred in our hostel, I decided to move out and take up temporary abode in one of the railroad station's depots, where I was working at the time. Most important, however, I made it my business to take a hot bath at least twice weekly in one of the city's bathing facilities.

Once, when I was just about to have one of my usual semi-weekly baths, I was told by the attendant to first hand in all my clothing for lice disinfection, *voshoboyka*, as it is called in Russian. I flatly refused to do so, but the man was firm in his demand. So I asked to see the manager of the establishment. As it happened, the manager turned out to be a young and energetic woman. When she asked why I refused to have my clothes disinfected, I replied that my previous experience with disinfection had been a very bad one, for after I handed in perfectly clean clothes, they were returned to me soiled and with a few lice on my shirt.

"How come?" inquired the manageress.

"Oh, it is very simple," I replied. "To make certain that all lice are killed off, you must run your disinfection installation at a temperature of over 100°C. This is essential for producing enough steam in the disinfection chamber. In addition, the process itself should last no less than half an hour, so that enough steam can penetrate through and through each and every item of clothing. But what happens here is that apparently your installation is being run at a lower temperature, producing little or no steam at all. Moreover, by cutting down the disinfection process to ten minutes or so, you fail to achieve the desired effect. And the result is just the opposite. Instead of killing the lice, you actually provide enough heat to keep them very much alive and for their larvas to develop more quickly."

"You seem to know quite a bit about these things," remarked the manageress. "Maybe you would like to work for us? Anyway, what is your present occupation?"

"Oh, I am just a railway porter," I answered, "but I do not intend to change my present job. All the same, thanks for your offer."

After that she proposed an arrangement by which my clothes would be deposited in her office each time I came to take a bath.

A week or so later, by chance, I came across my Russian friend, Leonid. As usual, I inquired about his well-being, and I also asked if any changes had been made in the hostel since I had left it. I was especially anxious to find out if any stricter precautionary measures had been taken after the death of the two refugees. And since we were discussing the subject of epidemics, I told Leonid about my latest experience in the city's bathing facility. Of course, I also related the conversation with the manageress and the subsequent arrangement regarding the disinfection of my clothing. In the end, I expressed my doubts to him as to whether the woman knew how to run a disinfection utility. When I finished, Leonid burst into laughter, saying that I must be very naive if I believed the manageress to be so innocent. From what he understood, it was quite obvious that part of the fuel required for running the installation was being stolen and probably sold on the black market, most certainly with the knowledge and consent of the manageress herself. I still had my doubts, until I met her again.

Once, after my usual bath, when I was just about to leave the place, the office door opened, and there stood the manageress. After we exchanged greetings, she hesitated for a while and then invited me into her office. Offering me a seat and a cigarette, she inquired whether I was satisfied with the arrangements she had made regarding my clothes. I answered that up to now I had no reason for any complaints. "If so," she said, "I have a business proposition for you. As you probably know, according to new regulations from the Ministry of Health, passengers are not allowed on or off the train without producing a valid disinfection treatment certificate. I should imagine that, as a porter working at the station, you are asked about the address of our facility. Instead of sending the people to our place, you could simply supply them with such a certificate on the spot for, let us say, thirty roubles apiece. This sum will then be split half and half between us for each blank certificate I supply you with," she concluded. At first, I was very much taken aback, almost shocked, by the unusual and bold proposition she made to me, an absolute stranger. But having regained my composure, I answered that I myself would not be interested in taking up her offer, since my earnings as a porter were quite good. Not discouraged by my refusal, and looking straight into my eyes all of a sudden, she asked me:

"What exactly is your nationality, if that is no secret?"

"Why do you want to know?" I asked her in return.

"Somehow, I thought you are Jewish," she said.

"Well, you were not mistaken," I answered. "I am Jewish. Is there anything wrong with being Jewish?"

"No, not at all! On the contrary, in the Soviet Union we do not differentiate between people because of their nationality," she replied.

"If so, why did you ask me at all?"

"Oh, I just wanted to be certain I could trust you," she answered.

"Well, now that you know you can't, surely there is no point in making me this offer, or is there?"

Not deterred by my refusal, she tried to convince me that there was no harm in earning some extra money, but I would not change my mind. So she suggested that I pass on the offer to someone else I knew well. The only condition she made was that the person should not be a local man. Though never intending to find someone else for the job, I promised to do my best.

Only after leaving her office did I fully realize the exact meaning of her *business* proposition. This was not merely an *innocent* way of getting around the Health Ministry's sanitary regulations. In fact, it was a criminal offense verging on health sabotage, for taking up her offer might have had much wider repercussions, affecting the very lives of a great number of innocent people. And all this because of a very prosaic and unbelievably simple reason. Had the Soviet authorities provided the population with a sufficient supply of soap and other cleaning materials in the first place, they would have limited, if not prevented, the spread of various diseases and epidemics. But paradoxically, as it turned out, they preferred tackling the problem in a centralized manner, that is, by building elaborate and expensive disinfection installations for the use of their citizens. However, because of a combination of psychological and technical reasons, these facilities proved largely ineffective. Moreover, by choosing a totalitarian way of caring for their people's well-being, the Soviet authorities deprived the ordinary citizen of the means of taking care of, and being responsible for, his or her own personal and general cleanliness, since cleanliness, as the very basis of a nation's health, depends first and foremost on each and every citizen.

* * *

Ending this unusual story, I find it necessary to point out that the manageress in question, the one who offered me such an "attractive" business proposition, was only one of many, many tens of millions of non-Jewish citizens, out of approximately 300,000,000 people, who populated the Soviet Union and for economic reasons were compelled to engage in black-marketeering. And what is true of the former Soviet Union is nowadays also true of any other country with an economy controlled by its government. Even countries with a free market economy are prone to develop a black market for particular goods or materials, should there be a demand for them, and the country in question, for reasons of its own, cannot or will not supply them. In the light of the above, is it not an abusive and vicious slander to blame the Jews for creating and running the black market?

5 The Blood Libel,
The Jewish Passover Festival,
And The Protestant Clergyman

One of the many unjust and baseless accusations held against the Jewish people for centuries has been the blood libel. Under it, Jews are still charged with kidnapping Christian children and, after murdering them, using their blood for religious rituals. According to one version of this fantastic tale, it is alleged that Christian blood is used by Jews for making *matzot*, unleavened bread, eaten during the festival of Passover, which commemorates the freeing of Jews from slavery in Egypt. In the past, this unbelievable but deliberate lie led to many accusations, based on the primitive but popular belief that Jews are possessed of some evil lust for murder, and that their bloodthirstiness springs from their hatred of mankind in general, and Christianity in particular.

As the Christian religion spread throughout Western Europe, it influenced people's emotions and sentiments even more than did thought and dogma. With the passage of time, many variations of this fantastic tale of the Jews' inhumanity and sadism began to multiply and spread. According to another version of this tale, as recounted by the Medieval monk and chronicler Matthew Paris: "The (kidnapped) child is first fattened for ten days with white bread and milk, and then killed." Furthermore, the same chronicler writes: "They (the Jews) kill Christian children, they torture them in all their limbs, and they take the blood to drink."

In the past, such unbelievable tales were spread by various popular preachers who instilled them in the minds of the common people. As a result, generation after generation of Jews in Europe were cruelly tortured, Jewish communities massacred, broken up and dispersed. In the nineteenth century, the hatred of Jews in its modern form of anti-Semitism used the blood libel for inciting ordinary people against the Jews. Often, the governments of various countries in Europe would exploit the blood libel to turn the attention of the masses from their own failure in coping with political, social and economic problems. Among many of the unjust Christian charges made against the Jews, the blood libel is the most sinister of all.

It was only in October 1965 that the Church officially repudiated many of the baseless accusations, including the blood libel, held against the Jewish people for centuries. However, exactly twenty-three years prior to that date a group of Jewish servicemen, including myself, went through a unique experience that once again disproved this fantastic allegation. Not only that, but contrary to all expectations, we were actually encouraged and officially helped to celebrate the Passover festival, though in a somewhat odd and rather irregular manner. All this happened aboard a troopship, while the Second

World War was in full progress, though we ourselves were far away from the fighting at the time.

Now, before I continue with my story, let me ask you this question: What would be your reaction if I told you that, because of a mistaken order given in the British army, some seventy Jewish servicemen aboard a ship were compelled to eat sweet biscuits with all their meals, instead of *matzot*, unleavened bread, as required during the Passover festival? And though this is in contravention of our Jewish religious dietary laws, we had no choice but to go through this ordeal for eight consecutive days, suffering from severe nausea and upset stomachs. Moreover, what would you say if I told you that of all people it was none other than a Protestant chaplain who had given the order? In the absence of a rabbi aboard the ship, the clergyman, acting in good faith but nevertheless mistakenly, had been responsible for this arrangement. Not only that; in his keen desire to comply with Jewish religious requirements, he also made certain that during the festival we abstained from eating any bread altogether. Thus, the devoted clergyman unwittingly also assumed the role of a religious supervisor, or *mashgiyah*, as he is called in Hebrew. No wonder, then, that to this day I cannot stand the very sight of biscuits, especially those looking pale and tasting like soap after prolonged storage. Here, then, is the rest of my story, in all its relevant detail.

On March 15, 1942, while the war was in full progress, the H.M.S. Straighthaird, then a troopship in the service of the British navy, had left Bombay for Port Elizabeth in South Africa. Aboard ship were about 2000 servicemen of different nationaliaties and armies. Among them was a contingent of 320 men belonging to the Polish Forces, at the time under British

Army Command. The final destination of all servicemen aboard the ship was Great Britain. Once there, we were to join our respective national armies, forming part of the future Allied Expeditionary Force. For security reasons, we had to take a roundabout route, zigzagging all the way in an attempt to avoid enemy torpedoes. Confined to a rather limited space aboard ship, we had to follow a rigid routine, partly because of cramped quarters, and partly because of limited hygienic facilities. The first part of our daily routine included morning deck parade, coupled with roll call, inspection, and reading out the order of the day. The latter also included the assignment of manpower for different duties aboard the ship. The second part of the day was usually taken up with talks and instructions on various military subjects, English language studies, entertainment, etc. In addition, from time to time, we were put through fire and lifeboat drill, making sure that all aboard know what to do in case of emergency.

It took us some time until we all became organized aboard the ship and settled down to a more or less fixed routine. Then, one morning towards the end of the deck-parade, we were told that those of us who followed the Jewish faith were to assemble the next day at 9 o'clock a.m. opposite the ship's chapel. Curious about the purpose of this meeting, we went to the appointed place the next morning somewhat earlier than required. At the chapel, some sixty or so coreligionists of different nationalities were already gathered, among them officers and all other ranks. Everyone present speculated as to the purpose of this gathering. At 9 o'clock sharp, very much to our surprise, there appeared a clergyman who introduced himself as Captain Robertson. "If you don't mind," said the clergyman, "please form a half circle, so that I can speak to you. Gentlemen!" he turned to us, "I am really sorry, but unfortunately there is no rabbi aboard this ship. And because of my position as chaplain, I have been given the task of looking after your religious requirements. I am not certain whether all of you are aware of the fact that the Passover festival falls tomorrow, the 14th of Nissan."

Pausing and checking our reaction to his announcement, the clergyman continued: "As you all know, there are certain religious requirements to be observed during the Passover festival, especially with regard to food. Therefore, I have arranged with the ship's Provisions Officer to make certain changes in your daily food ration, for the duration of the festival. As I understand, you are not allowed to eat any bread during the eight days of Passover. Unfortunately, we cannot provide you with *matzot*, or unleavened bread, as required, and therefore you will be supplied with an equivalent ration of biscuits. Similarly, instead of the necessary wine, you will be getting a daily allocation of rum. And, as far as work is concerned, starting from tomorrow, you will be free from all daily chores for the duration of the Passover festival."

Stopping again for a moment to observe our reaction to his arrangements, the chaplain continued: "If there is anyone among you who is able to organize and conduct a religious service, I will be glad to put our chapel at your disposal. Should you decide to do so, however, we would have to choose different hours for our respective services, so that they won't clash. Now, gentlemen, if you have any questions to ask, I will do my best to answer them." After a short silence, the clergyman continued: "I understand that you have no questions, so I take this opportunity to wish you a happy Passover. May you all survive the war and return safely and in good health to your families and friends. God bless you!" proclaimed the genial chaplain, ending his speech.

We had no questions to ask and there was no volunteer to conduct a public religious service in the chapel. How could anyone reconcile the best intentions of a Protestant clergyman with the contradictory basics of the Jewish faith? Our daily allocation of rum did not exactly fulfill the role of wine required for the religious ceremony at the Passover table. Nonetheless, it proved a welcome means of enhancing the appetites of those very few of us who could still stomach the midday meal of corned beef with mashed potatoes that was served to us almost each day during our long voyage. As to biscuits, they totally failed to meet our religious requirements, for the simple reason that biscuits are made of dough containing yeast. And any food, whether baked or cooked, containing yeast is strictly forbidden during the Jewish Passover. Even apart from religious considerations, on normal days sweet biscuits could never be a suitable substitute for good, ordinary, everyday bread. This is especially true if you happen to be an East European and are used to having bread not only with every meal, but practically with every course.

No wonder, then, that after eight days of such an ordeal, many of us developed stomach trouble and were glad to go back to our daily ration of bread, as soon as the Passover festival was over. Nevertheless, all of us were very grateful to the well-disposed chaplain, who went to so much trouble to make all the necessary preparations, even though they did not exactly meet our religious needs.

I should like to point out here that all those arrangements made by the ship's chaplain were against the wishes and without the approval of the Polish officer in charge of our contingent. At first, the officer argued that because of the war, the whole idea of organizing our Passover celebrations was inappropriate and even wrong. But having failed to convince the British clergyman, the officer tried to influence him to give up the idea of freeing us from daily duties aboard the ship during the festival. The reason the officer gave was that freeing us from work would cause discontent, even friction between the non-Jewish and Jewish servicemen of our contingent. But again, the clergyman would not give in, arguing that had there been a Christian holiday, he would require the Jewish servicemen to fulfill their daily duties aboard the vessel without any excuses. In any case, said the chaplain, since our contingent now came under British jurisdiction, he was obliged to act according to British army regulations. But, perhaps, the most grotesque part of it all was the fact that in my official capacity as English interpreter, despite being Jewish, I had to serve as intermediary between the Protestant chaplain and the Catholic officer, who did not speak English. However, this is not the end of the whole story.

Some four years or so later, I took a month's leave from the army to travel from Scotland to England. While in London, I came across a notice in one of the daily newspapers that soldiers on active duty could send parcels of food and clothing to their relatives in Germany. I had a brother there, an ex-prisoner of a German camp in New Ulm. I wanted to send him a parcel, but could do so only through a special Soldiers' Welfare Committee. In search of the address of such an institution, I was told by a friend that a welfare committee operated within the London-based Jewish Agency. Wasting no time, I decided to go there. Climbing up the stairs of the building on Great Russell Street, where the Agency was located at the time, I bumped into a man carrying a huge bundle of used clothing. Next to him was a clergyman, apparently his employer, who was giving him instructions where to deposit the bundle. At first, I did not pay much attention to the two men, but standing in line for the receiving clerk, I heard the clergyman speak again. This time his voice seemed to me somewhat familiar. Trying hard to recall where and when I had ever heard that voice, it suddenly dawned on me that it must be the good old chaplain. Uncertain and somewhat hesitant, I approached the clergyman and asked him if by any chance he happened to be Captain Robertson of the H.M.S. Straighthaird:

"Yes," he replied, "I am Captain Robertson, but who are you?"

"Well," I answered, "I am one of those chaps you had put through an eight-day ordeal of eating corned beef with sweet biscuits, and drinking rum instead of wine."

At first, he looked at me somewhat puzzled. But when I mentioned to him more details of his Passover arrangements aboard the ship, he smiled broadly, recollecting the whole event. Later, when I said goodbye to this genial clergyman, he thanked me for setting him straight regarding some baffling customs of the Jewish religion.

* * *

The above, then, is the truth, nothing but the naked truth, about the whole Passover ritual, as observed by a group of Jewish servicemen during World War II. As we have seen, it was organized and supervised not by a rabbi, but a Protestant clergyman, "for a change," aboard the H.M.S. Straighthaird, one of the ships in the service of the Royal Navy.

6 From Borrowing Money At Exorbitant Interest Rates To Supplementing Army Pay By Moonlighting

Among the negative portrayals of the medieval Jew was also that of the moneylender, accused of charging exorbitant interest. In this context, however, it is important to point out that owing to the social and economic conditions prevailing in medieval Christian Europe, Jews were compelled to engage in this much-despised occupation for two main reasons. One was that because of various legal limitations, Jews were restricted in their trading activities, prohibited from owning land, and barred from belonging to any of the existing craft and trade guilds.

The other reason, a more significant one, was that the medieval canon law of the Church had forbidden Christians to engage in lending money with interest. Restricted in earning a livelihood, a Jew could only engage in either limited trading or money lending. And since the various feudal states and the Church itself could not manage their own finances without outside assistance, Jews conveniently fulfilled that function. Encouraged by inducements to engage in money lending, they were granted certain privileges and protection by various kings, princes, landlords and clerics.

At the same time, Jews were also exposed to dangerous practices by some of their unscrupulous debtors. Whenever money was due by such a debtor, he would often avoid payment by some trivial excuse, and have the moneylender either imprisoned or murdered. Despite the fact that the Jews fulfilled an important economic function in medieval Christian Europe, and contributed greatly to the future development of the banking system, they were, nevertheless, regarded as parasites and exploiters of the Christian population. And because of that, they suffered not only acts of humiliation, but also abuse and physical harm.

From the historical point of view, the year 1290 was an important date in the lives of English and European Jews. That year marked the expulsion of Jews from England under Edward I. This came about not only as a result of the prolonged condemnation of the Jews by the church, but mainly in order to appease the anger and hatred of the various debtors in his kingdom, who could not and would not discharge all their debts. Of course, it goes without saying that, before the expulsion, the property belonging to the Jews was confiscated and the borrowers' debts revoked. But since then seven hundred or so years have elapsed, and during that period providence – or should I say a twist of fate – changed the once-established order. It turned the proverbial role of the Christian borrower to a moneylender and that of a Jew to be his debtor, as, indeed, also happened in my own case. There is, however, one fundamental difference. While in the past Jews had been greatly abused and condemned for pursuing money-lending activities, their contemporary Christian counterparts suffer no such humiliation or physical harm.

Here, then, is my account of how we ordinary soldiers of the Polish Forces, based in Scotland during World War II, fell into the hands of unscrupulous non-Jewish moneylenders. Put on reduced army pay through no fault of our own, we turned to borrowing money to supplement our meager income. The only possible source we could tap for loans were our own immediate superiors. They were ready and more than willing to serve as our moneylenders, but demanded to be paid exorbitant rates of interest on all our loans. But when, after a certain time, our indebtedness to our superiors reached critical proportions, we decided to rebel.

Our rebellion took a rather unconventional form, however, contrary to the usual practice of resisting authority by disobeying orders. To make up for the lost pay, we decided to engage in moonlighting, apart from and in addition to our regular duties and other army obligations. For the background and conditions that led to this extraordinary development, it is necessary to take you back to the very beginning of this unusual story and tell you about it in greater detail.

Those of us who served in the Polish Forces under British command during the Second World War were entitled to receive the same pay as British servicemen. However, in spite of this official regulation, we actually got less, but not because of any fault on the part of the British Army Paymaster's office. The reason for our reduced remuneration was that the Polish army had a larger number of officers than stipulated by British army manpower standards. To keep these officers on the army's payroll, an internal source of financing had to be found. And so, to solve the problem, our military authorities decided on a simple, but nevertheless unjust, solution. Instead of issuing our pay every seven days, or once a week, as British army regulations provided, this was done every ten days, or only three times a month instead of four. The money thus saved went to defray the salaries of those extra officers kept on our staff.

That solution, apart from being unjust, left many of us with very little cash to spend. To make matters worse, the pay of soldiers from other Allied countries, such as Canada, New Zealand and Australia, not to speak of the United States of America, was not just higher than ours, but more than double what we were receiving. For they were paid by both the British and their own respective governments. One can justly claim that of all the Allied forces we, soldiers of the Polish army, were the most poorly paid. No wonder, then, that apart from feeling envious and dissatisfied, most of us found it difficult to make ends meet. We often had to resort to borrowing money

Now, the only people in the army who could possibly meet our financial needs were our own direct superiors, namely the non-commissioned officers. As already mentioned, they were ready and more than willing to do so, but demanded to be paid a disproportionally high rate of interest. Each payday, the borrowed money plus exorbitant interest would be reimbursed, but after a few days, with our cash gone, we would have to borrow again. And so for months, payday in and payday out, every ten days or so, the cycle would be repeated.

Apart from moral considerations, this system of borrowing money was bound to have a detrimental effect on army discipline, especially since the vast majority of ordinary servicemen were depending for extra cash on a small minority of their direct superiors. And may I say that all those superiors who engaged in money-lending as a profitable sideline were not very scrupulous in all their dealings with us, to say the least. As for myself, I pretty soon came to the conclusion that, in order to avoid getting into a deeper mess, I had to break out of this vicious circle as quickly as possible. Fortunately, such an opportunity came along when I was transferred to another unit.

My new base, the Polish Training Signal Corps Center, located in a small place called Achtermuchty, near the Scottish township of Kirkaldy, proved to be a well organized and smoothly running establishment. One part of the center was responsible for training officers and other ranks, whilst the other part of the establishment operated a number of communications equipment repair shops. Having settled down to my new job as a radio technician, I discovered very soon that some of the workshops were doing work not only for the army, but also for the private benefit of those who were running them. In fact, these workshops were producing various articles sought by servicemen which, at the time, could not be bought in the shops or on the open market. Cigarette lighters, bracelets, wristlets, medallions, etc., were the most popular, but also photo albums, valises, ladies' handbags, and other similar items, were in great demand. These articles were sold directly for hard cash to the servicemen for their girl friends, acquaintances, and others. Sometimes, though not often, business was also done with the local population, but mostly on a barter basis in which money was not involved. I should like to point out that all this activity, though illegal as such, helped us not only to supplement our reduced army pay, without resorting to any loans at exorbitant interest rates, but also filled the vacuum created by the war for these, as well as many other articles.

Returning to the question of usury in the Middle Ages, it is important to point out that the expansion of trade and industry during the centuries that followed, especially with the beginning of the Industrial Revolution, demanded increased credit and, therefore, a modification of the attitude towards money-lending activities. Usury, then, as a term, came to be applied only to exorbitant or unreasonable rates of interest, charged over and above what was regarded as a fair premium.

Nowadays, however, the practice of setting legal rates of interest has been adopted by most financial institutions throughout the western world. These rates are based on the economic principle of supply and demand for all monies circulating at any given time in a particular country, as controlled and regulated by its central bank. In practice, however, the old concept of usury has simply changed form. Instead of the individual moneylender of the medieval past, nowadays the governments of most countries practice the modern concept of usury. By running inflationary economies, they constantly depreciate the value of their currencies, thereby diminishing the real worth of their people's wages, salaries and savings. In some countries, the rate of inflation reaches such high proportions that ordinary citizens are being constantly pauperized by their own governments. However, while in the past Jews had been condemned and greatly abused for pursuing various financial activities, nowadays members of the governments concerned suffer no such humiliation or physical harm.

7 Why Do Jews Marry Outside Their Faith, And Do They Make Better Husbands Than Their Gentile Counterparts

For many centuries, the Justinian Code of the Roman Empire, and the canon laws of the Catholic Church, regulated the lives of the Jewish people in Europe. In addition, various medieval rulers, feudal princes, landlords, as well as the local governments of many provinces and boroughs, frequently issued discriminatory decrees and regulations of their own, affecting their Jewish residents. One of many such derogatory and especially insulting canons enacted by the Catholic Church required that Jews and Christians be kept apart. Therefore, no Jew could live with a Christian in the same house, share a meal with him, or maintain any social contact. For the same reason, no Christian servant, or wet-nurse (a woman employed to breast-feed another woman's baby) could be employed in a Jewish household. Most significant of all, however, was the strict prohibition of mixed marriages between Christians and Jews. The purpose of all those canons, as stated, was "to protect

Christians from all wicked influences that Jews exert on Christian society."

In a later period, the third and fourth Lateran Church Councils, held in 1179 and 1215 respectively, not only promulgated the existing decree of separation between Christians and Jews, but also reinforced it and extended it to include further limitations. From then on, Jews had to wear different and distinctive clothing, so as to be easily recognizable. As a result, they became the target of unwarranted harassment and abuse. In addition, the aforementioned Lateran Councils decreed that, in any lawsuit brought by a Jew against a Christian, the testimony of a Christian witness was to be preferred to that of a Jew. Jews could not employ Christian domestics, and any Christian who disregarded this prohibition was liable to be excommunicated. Similarly, the use of a Jewish physician's services by a Christian required the person's confession and penance. In general, a Jew could not hold any public office. But if appointed to such a post, he was pressured and compelled to undergo conversion with or without his consent.

Many of the anti-Jewish decrees and limitations referred to, as well as new ones enacted throughout the centuries, were enforced with various degrees of severity, depending on the period, the country, and its ruler or regime. Some accusations and practices, especially the more sinister ones, such as the blood libel, the ghetto, and the wearing of the yellow badge – the "Badge of Shame," as it was called – survived and continued to be applied in the twentieth century with extreme brutality by the Nazis and their supporters. Certain canons, however, such as mixed marriages between Christians and Jews, despite their strict prohibition by the Church, have since been disregarded. There is an illustrative example.

One of the many curiosities I came up against during my stay in Great Britain was the widely accepted notion that, for some reason or other, Jews make better husbands than their gentile counterparts. Somewhat intrigued by this assertion, I wondered where it came from and what its basis was. For as far as I knew, it was true rather of Jewish women, who have the reputation of being exceptionally good mothers, and very often, though not always, devoted wives. But the claim that Jews make better husbands than do gentile menfolk was, at the time, a puzzle to me. If anything, some of the facts pointed to the contrary. This was especially true in pre-war Eastern Europe and, after World War II, in many western countries also.

As has been well known since time immemorial, man's task has been to be the family's main provider, while that of a woman to take care of the household and children. However, among some Jewish married couples, especially the very religious ones, this division of tasks either does not exist at all, or, if it does, is usually disproportionately divided between husband and wife – and almost always to the disadvantage of the latter.

It is the custom and the pride of every ultra-religious Jewish family to have at least one of its members engaged in the study of the Torah, the Holy Scriptures, daily from early morning until late at night. As a result, that person is prevented from doing any work. The burden of providing for such a family, in addition to managing a household, falls mainly on the shoulders of the Torah scholar's wife. She is compelled to do this by engaging in some profitable work or employment.

Often, although not necessarily always, such a couple is also helped financially by close relatives, usually their parents. With regard to other, ordinary Jewish married couples, whenever the husband is not the sole provider, his wife shares with him the burden of catering to the family's needs very much in the same manner as non-Jewish married couples do.

To find out what caused British women to accord Jewish husbands such a rare and distinctive quality, I decided to investigate the matter. The subject of my inquiry were young, middle-aged, as well as elderly women, both single and married, stemming from various walks of life, whom I had come across during my stay in Great Britain. I put two questions to all of them: Why do Jews marry outside their faith, and do they make better husbands than their gentile counterparts? Out of some thirty women I had interviewed, practically none could or would answer the first of my questions. As regards to the second, only two of the women interviewed gave negative answers, and one was undecided. The other women replied in the affirmative, giving various reasons to support their claim.

Some women asserted that a Jewish married man seldom frequents bars, nightclubs, or places of dubious repute. Also, they said, a Jewish married man usually stays away from everyday "boozing," and thus saves not only time and money, but also preserves his health for his own, as well as his family's sake. Most importantly, however, they emphasized the fact that seldom, if at all, would he get sufficiently drunk to cause harm to his wife, children and property.

Other women maintained that, as a rule, a Jewish husband is a reliable and responsible partner. This, they said, is especially true with regard to the way he manages his earnings.

Most, if not all of it, is spent on providing for and taking care of his family's needs. And if he possesses some weaknesses, like betting on horse and dog races, or football games, as most men do, it is usually for fun and very seldom, if at all, gambling without restraint.

Some other women declared that in most cases the average Jewish male is educated, enterprising, and ambitious to succeed in life. As a rule, they claimed, he spends most of his free time with wife, children and relatives. In short, he prefers home life to outside enjoyments. And because of all these qualities, they maintained, he definitely makes a good family man.

Overwhelmed by such unexpected and one-sided results to my inquiry, I tried to probe into the matter, so as to get a more balanced view of a Jewish husband's qualities. To my surprise, I was given an opposite view by my own landlady. When asked about her opinion on the matter, she contradicted all the positive qualities named by the majority of women I interviewed on the subject. Using an example, she explained to me that there are twenty-four hours in a day-and-night cycle, and that they can be split into three equal parts: eight hours for rest and sleep; eight hours for doing work, and eight hours for recreation and enjoyment. But, she said, "our men are spoiled by the government, which is paying them unemployment money, and giving other financial assistance in cases of redundancy. Therefore, when employed," she added, "they try not to overwork themselves. Instead, they take longer hours for recreation and enjoyment, always at the expense of their rest and sleep, and, if they manage, their work, too."

"But the Jews, the Jews," she repeated, "they are bastards. They sleep fewer hours, spend less time enjoying themselves, if at all, but work harder and longer hours, and make a lot of money. This is why our women are after them."

"Are you quite sure those are the only reasons for their being prefered?" I asked my landlady.

"Of course," she replied, "what other reasons could there be?"

"I don't know," I said, "maybe it is because they are more macho, and that is why they succeed where others fail."

"What do you mean by macho?" she asked me, somewhat puzzled.

"What I mean is that they are more manly, that is what I mean," I answered.

"How should I know? I have never yet slept with a Jew!" she retorted angrily.

"Well, if you hurry up, you may still have a chance. Better late than never," I snapped back, ending our conversation.

Whatever the reasons, there is no doubt that more and more gentile women, especially Christian women in Great Britain and some other western countries, tend to marry Jewish males. And since the Second World War this process, as shown by statistics, is steadily on the increase. Having more or less satisfied myself as to the reasons for this phenomenon, as far as gentile women were concerned, I was now anxious to find out what prompts Jewish males to respond in such increased numbers to the charm and attraction of non-Jewish women.

It so happened that, at the time I conducted this inquiry, by chance I met the Secretary of the Jewish Institute in Scotland. In the course of our conversation, I mentioned the results of my private investigation and asked him if he could assist me with any other information on the subject. I was especially anxious to receive statistical and other relevant data with regard to Jewish males. For some unknown reason, he would not promise to provide me with any written material, but otherwise was quite willing and ready to help me with my inquiry. When I visited the man in his office the next day, he told me the following: Strictly speaking, there are four, or rather five, main reasons why Jews tend to marry gentile women. Referring to the Encyclopaedia Judaica, he named them as follows:

One reason Jews marry outside their faith depends on the "Social Factors Related to Intermarriage. Romantic Love Versus Group Cohesion. In the western world, the selection of marital partners is governed by two considerations. One is the romantic love ideal, which tends to override considerations of race, creed, cultural origin, or social class. The other consideration is group survival, the pressure to marry a member of one's own race, religion, or cultural group. Elopements can be considered extreme cases of romantic love, producing a maximum rate of intermarriage, while arranged marriages can be viewed as a most conscious effort to foster group survival generating a minimum of such marriages."

Another reason for intermarriage depends on the size of the Jewish Community, its density and concentration. It has been repeatedly observed that the rate of intermarriage is the result of density, the proportion that a subgroup constitutes of the total population in a given locality. However, density becomes relevant only when the will for group survival has been weakened or abandoned. Once group cohesion is weakened, the factor of density operates in the expected manner: the smaller the proportion that Jews constitute of the total population in a given locality, the higher the intermarriage rate becomes."

Still another reason for Jews marrying outside their faith, he explained, depends on the "Age of Jewish Settlement and Democratic Social Process. Jews more than any other religious-ethnic group have been involved in migrations from one country to another. As immigrants they have encountered economic, cultural, and social barriers. However, in democratic societies, where equalizing processes between immigrants and older settlers and between different racial, ethnic, and religious groups are at least not discouraged, and at best consciously fostered, these barriers will be lowered with increasing length of settlement. In time, then, the Jews will become 'acculturated,' i.e., less distinguishable from older settlers and other immigrant groups. The most significant break in cultural continuity, social distance, and personal identity occurs with the birth of each new generation. Therefore, intermarriage is likely to increase with increased length of Jewish settlement, as measured by generations, and in the absence of continued Jewish immigration."

A further reason for Jewish intermarriage depends on their "Occupation and Employment Status. Occupation and employment status (independent owner versus employee) are factors significantly related to intermarriage. As long as occupational choice was limited by discriminatory practices, occupational homogeneity discouraged intermarriage. With virtually unlimited freedom of occupational choice as, for instance, in the United States, individuals who break away from traditional occupations are likely to have a higher intermarriage rate. The growth of corporate capitalism is also likely to generate a higher rate of intermarriage. Since large corporations demand from their executives considerable geographic and social mobility, local ties to the organized Jewish communities become attenuated."

An additional reason influencing mixed marriages is "Religious education. There is a widespread belief that Jewish education, including a bar mitzvah ceremony (attaining religious adulthood), helps to keep young men from marrying outside the Jewish faith. The Greater Washington survey showed that this belief is well founded, as far as the native-born of native parentage (the third and subsequent generations) is concerned. Religious education cut the intermarriage status rate in half. Since ethnic bonds – expressed in secular activities and in a common language – have been virtually dissolved in the third generation, exposure to religious instruction, which usually includes some learning of Jewish history and some identification with Israel, serves as a check to intermarriage."

But, unexpectedly, the most common reason for intermarriage, given to me by the Secretary of the Jewish Institute, was the fact that practically the majority of Jewish males who marry out of their faith do so because they simply fall in love with the woman of their choice. This romantic approach tends to override all other considerations such as race, religion, cultural origin, or the social class of the women in question. By the way, out of the thirty or so gentile women I had interviewed on the subject, only five mentioned love as a valid enough reason for wanting to marry a Jewish male. In this context, I would like to make two observations.

The first is that when a Jew marries a Jewish woman he expects and also receives a dowry. This widely spread practical approach to marriage does, of course, in no way preclude the element of love. But when a Jewish male marries a gentile women, he usually neither expects nor receives any dowry at all. However, that would not necessarily be the case, should the woman in question marry a gentile man instead of a Jewish male.

The second observation is that, if the findings of my inquiry are correct, it follows that gentile women marry Jewish males mainly, though not solely, for their personal qualities and material security. When a Jew marries a gentile woman, however, he does so mainly because he has fallen in love with her, pure and simple. If that is the case – and there is no reason to believe the contrary – it follows that the widespread notion about Jews doing everything in life solely for the sake of material gain is a shameful and groundless fallacy.

One day at tea time, my landlady asked me all of a sudden about the results of my inquiry, which I had already completed and filed away for future reference. Unwilling to be drawn into a futile discussion, I tried to evade her question. However, since she would not be easily dissuaded, I had no choice but to go into details, explaining to her the results of my study. When I finished, she made the following comment: "That our women marry Jews for money, I knew all along and I told you so, didn't I? But that Jews fall in love with our women, I would have never, never believed it!"

"But now that you know the facts, surely there is nothing to prevent you from having a go at it yourself, or is there?" I asked jokingly of my widowed landlady. "After all, as you can see, Jewish men do it out of love and not for the sake of money!"

And so, who said that Jews are not sentimental and always follow reason and not their emotions?

8 A Jewish Husband From Europe For A Millionaire's Daughter In South Africa

One of the most serious problems facing the Jewish people in the world today is their deficient natural increase in proportion to, and as compared with, other nations. Such a negative demographic development is highly detrimental to the future survival of any nation, but especially the Jews, who lost over six million people as a result of the Holocaust. In 1939, just before the outbreak of World War II, there were some 17 million Jews in the world. However, since then, during a period of some fifty-five years, the Jewish population has been reduced to about 14 million. In global terms, this means that the number of Jews has come down from about one per cent to less than one third of one percent in proportion to the total world population.

It may be of interest here to note that, during the same period, some of the former belligerents such as Germany, Japan, and Russia, particularly Germany and Russia, which lost many millions of people during World War II, managed not only to make up their population losses, but also to substantially increase their total numbers. On the other hand, the comparatively small increase in Diaspora Jews – those residing outside of Israel – who during more than half a century have failed even so much as to bring their numbers to the pre-war level, is indeed a most disturbing symptom. Advanced aging, assimilation, and particularly a high percentage of intermarriage are factors explaining this limited natural increase. Hence, the demographic future of the Jews in the world is indeed in great jeopardy. While various measures such as religious instruction, Jewish education, social and cultural activities, etc., are being employed to arrest this tendency, there is really no substitute for the preservation of the Jewish people, aside from those appropriate steps, that each and every Jewish family can take, as the following story will reveal.

Have you ever wondered why on earth a young soldier, on short leave from the army, would decide to visit, of all places, a local dolphinarium early on a Sunday morning? Well, the answer is that most likely he may do so when he finds himself with plenty of time on his hands, but with nothing else to do and nowhere else to go. And so, to kill time, he chooses to spend the whole morning either at a museum, or an art gallery, or some other similar touring site. This assertion is only valid until, later in the day, some other recreational and entertainment facilities in town become available.

Now, that is exactly what happened to me and a soldier friend of mine when, on a short leave from our unit, we went to visit the famous Durban Dolphinarium. While walking from one aquarium to another, observing the great variety of fish species, I could not but recall my childhood years, when I was first introduced to the world of fauna, but mainly by means of pictures in my school textbooks. But here in South Africa, one could watch and admire these creatures in their true size in the very country of their natural habitat.

After walking around for three hours or so, we became somewhat tired, and I suggested to my friend that we take a break and have a snack in one of the dolphinarium's cafeterias. But my friend, who from the very beginning was against the whole idea of going to the dolphinarium, was fed up. Impatient with this childish pursuit, as he called it, he suddenly shouted in anger – for some unknown reason in Russian: "I tell you, enough is enough! Let's leave this place and go back to town!" While arguing with him to delay our departure, I heard from behind my back someone ask in a pleasant voice:

"Do you fellows speak Russian?"

"Yes, sure we do," I replied, and turning around, I saw two young fairly good-looking women in their very early twenties. "Why do you ask?" I inquired.

"Well," answered one of them, "originally our father came from Russia, and he would be very happy to meet people who speak Russian."

Though my friend urged me to leave, I was willing to take a chance and wait to meet their father. Eventually the young women and I convinced my friend to stay on, and we all decided to go and have some refreshments. From our conversation with them, we learned that the two women were sisters, students at Durban University. Jennifer, the older, was studying medicine, while her younger sister, Eleanor, had taken up sociology. Their father, they explained, had fled Russia just before the October Revolution in 1917, and together with his family had settled in South Africa. Also, it turned out that the two sisters lived with their parents at Clairwoods, a posh suburb of Durban, about ten miles from where our camp was located.

Engrossed in conversation with the two sisters, we hardly noticed a man who stopped at our table.

"Hello!" he greeted us cheerfully. "My name is Mr. J., and I am the father of the two young ladies in your company." Pulling up a chair, he sat down at our table. "Are you not going to introduce me to your friends?" Mr. J. asked his daughters.

"Certainly, father," replied Jennifer. "But guess what surprise we have in store for you!"

"Surprise?" repeated Mr. J., "what surprise? I hope you are not going to keep me in suspense, or are you?"

"No, father," replied Jennifer, "our friends speak Russian."

"Did you say Russian? Well, well, if that is so, I am sure your friends won't refuse to have dinner with us at our place," Mr. J. concluded.

We arrived at Mr. J.'s residence late in the afternoon and were introduced to his wife and other members of the family. After the introductions, the sisters suggested that we look around their mansion and its grounds. Though elegant family houses are by no means scarce in South Africa, one would have to admit that theirs was exceptionally handsome. The well-planned and spacious building, surrounded by a large and beautifully laid out garden and many lawns, had all the necessary facilities for recreation and sports. In short, one could easily gauge that its residents were not only rich, but also people who knew how to combine modesty with good taste. After an hour or so spent in the grounds of their residence, we heard the sound of a gong. This was to let us know that dinner was about to be served. Hurrying back to the mansion, we first went to refresh ourselves before sitting down for dinner.

Mr. J., who was already waiting for us in the dining room, seated himself comfortably at the head of the table. With a hospitable gesture he invited us to take our places, making sure that each of us took a chair opposite one of his daughters. Mrs. J., as befits the lady of the house, took a seat at the other end of the table, facing her husband.

The convention was such, that each time Mrs. J. rang a bell, a kitchen maid would enter the dining room, pushing a trolley with several bowls of food in front of her. These were put on a small table, and from it Mrs. J. would dish the food onto our plates.

Throughout the meal, Mr. J. appeared to be in excellent humor, full of spirit. He cracked jokes all the time and told us funny stories about his early experiences in South Africa After two meat appetizers, we were served soup. And it was while I was eating my soup, that Mr. J. turned to me suddenly and, speaking in Russian, said: "Listen Henry! How would you like to marry one of my daughters?" On hearing his unexpected and direct proposition, I unwittingly dropped my spoon, feeling utterly embarrassed and confused. Mrs. J., who seemingly did not understand Russian, asked me if there was anything wrong with the soup. "Of course not," I replied, having regained my composure. "Apparently," I explained, "a few drops of soup must have entered my windpipe, causing me some discomfort." But soon the whole incident was forgotten, and we continued with our meal as if nothing had happened.

After dinner my friend left Mr. J.'s residence, excusing himself under some pretext, but not without first thanking our hosts for their hospitality. Abandoned by my friend, I was now left on my own to face Mr. J. who, after the meal, suggested that we have a cigar in the adjacent smoking-room. Having comfortably settled himself in one of the easy chairs, he invited me to take a seat opposite him. After lighting his cigar, and exchanging a few polite phrases, Mr. J. repeated his previous proposition. This time, however, he did so in English, and in a somewhat less direct manner, adding that he was a little surprised at my embarrassment at the table. But now, with no other member of his family present, I told Mr. J. that, strictly speaking, it was I who should be surprised at his rather unconventional, direct approach to such a delicate and serious matter as marriage. First, because he did not know me or my background well enough to come up with such a proposition; secondly, as a soldier on active duty, in time of war, my intentions and decisions were rather limited, to say the least. I also explained to Mr. J. that there was very little, if anything, I could offer, or possessed, apart, perhaps, from the uniform I was wearing at the time. But even that, I humorously pointed out, did not belong to me, but to His Majesty's Forces. Perhaps the most important question of all was, what made him so certain that one of his daughters would be interested in marrying me?

For a few moments Mr. J. kept silent, probably thinking how he should respond to my queries; then, looking straight into my eyes, he said:

"Young man, what I am now going to tell you may not exactly sound like straightforward answers to your questions. But when you hear my personal story, I am sure you will understand the reason for my proposition."

After pausing for a moment and taking a deep breath, Mr. J. continued:

"A very short time before the Russian Revolution in 1917, my family came to settle in South Africa. We had no money, we didn't know the language of the country, and there was nobody who could possibly help us to get settled. So, at the early age of fourteen, I began working at various jobs – first as an errand boy and then as a peddler for a local firm. After three years or so, I became a salesman for a large foreign concern. And at the age of twenty-four I already owned a business of my own. Four years later, I took over two competing firms dealing in the same commodities as me. Before the age of thirty-six, I branched out and became an industrialist, manufacturing goods for my own shops as well as for other outlets. For the last fifteen years or so, as an industrialist, I have continued expanding all my existing enterprises, acquiring, from time to time, new ones as well. Today, I am well established and control directly or indirectly a number of companies, with a total turnover in millions.

"All this wealth I have acquired by working very hard during these long years, putting in sixteen and often more hours of work each day. However, I will be sixty years old soon, and I think it is just about the right time for a younger man to gradually take over part of my business responsibilities. Surely," stressed Mr. J., "it is the most natural thing in the world to want to transfer some of these tasks to a person who also happens to be the husband of my own daughter."

I listened attentively to Mr. J.'s story, and when he finished I noticed that my host's face was covered with heavy sweat. Somehow, despite his apparent achievements and success in business, I could sense a feeling of pain, or even grief, when he was recounting his life story to me. Maybe, I thought, this was due to the fact that Mr. J. had no male heir of his own, who could succeed him in the firm. On the other hand, there may have been some other reasons, too. Anyway, it took me a while until I found the right words to reply to Mr. J. I told him that I was deeply touched and honored by the confidence he seemed to have in me. I then expressed my conviction that there must be a number of local young men of Jewish stock, better known to him than to me, who could meet all his requirements. Some of them, I added, might even already be established businessmen and, apart from bringing their professional experience, could also add to his family's wealth.

Now came Mr. J.'s turn to speak again, and this is what he said to me:

"My friend, you are quite right in saying that there are a number of educated young men who could and, I am pretty sure, would, very much want to marry into my family. But the danger is that with a liberal education in this country, either of my daughters might easily marry a non-Jew, and that would be a real disaster for me and my wife. Not that I am in any way religious or conservative in my thinking. But the fact is that I come from a family that produced generations of rabbis, and should any of my children marry out of the faith, it would be a real tragedy for all of us. But even if the prospective husbands are of Jewish stock, they would belong to the second or even third generation of people born in this country. Most of them are used to a good, easy life. Should either of my daughters marry a local man, I very much fear that, instead of preserving my family's wealth, he would not overexert himself in achieving this goal, and that is at best. And at worst," he emphasized, "in no time he may even dissipate everything I built up over these years. That is why I would like to see my daughters married to Jewish men from Europe, especially the part that you and I come from. People like us," said Mr. J., "still have enough ambition and driving force to make good in life.

"Now," said Mr. J., "let me make a suggestion. If my information is correct, you are going to stay in this country for another six to eight weeks, until such time as a ship becomes available to take you to Britain. During that period you will have plenty of time to consider my proposition, without any obligation whatsoever. And in the meantime, whenever you feel like coming to visit us, you will always be a welcome guest in our house. And this applies to your friend as well," concluded Mr. J.

It was almost midnight when I said goodbye to Mr. J. and his family and was driven back to camp. But that night I could not fall asleep, as I was still under the impact of Mr. J.'s unusual proposition. I must confess it took me a few days to make up my mind, to accept his non-obligatory suggestion, though not without hesitation and some misgivings.

For practical reasons, I had first to convince my friend and get him to agree to share with me the company of the two sisters. I did that only after diplomatically securing their consent. Following that, my friend and I became frequent visitors at their house. And so, when on leave from camp, we would spend most of our free time with the two sisters, going out together to many social events, and enjoying one another's company. Every so often, Mrs. J. would insist that we stay at their house and have dinner with the rest of the family. Of course, at those times Mr. J. would have an opportunity to speak Russian with us. The two sisters, apart from being quite attractive, also proved to be intelligent and well-read. Therefore, the time we spent in their company was always very pleasant and most gratifying. During the eight weeks or so of our stay in South Africa, we enjoyed ourselves thoroughly.

Then, one evening after dinner at their house, when I was on my own again, Mr. J. suggested that we go into the smoking room for the usual chat and cigar. Inviting me to take a seat, he turned to me, and in a somewhat solemn voice said:

"Well, Henry, I have news for you. In a couple of days or so, the H.M.S. Anglia is due here from Bombay. She is to take aboard some 750 servicemen destined for Britain. Somehow, I have a hunch that this time your group will be among them. However, the truth is that during the two months or so that you boys have been here, we have all become very much attached to you. It is also my impression that during this period you, too, managed to get on especially well with my younger daughter, Eleanor, and if I am not mistaken, not without reciprocity on her part. Now, if you will remember my proposition and accept it – this is the time to act."

The truth is, during all that time, I was aware of the fact that our stay in South Africa was only temporary. I am sure Mr. J. must have been, too. One day we would have to leave the country. Because of this, I hoped that he would not bring up his marriage proposition again, especially since I had given him my reasons against it. But now, pressed for an answer and not wanting to offend Mr. J., I told him that my friend and I very much appreciated the hospitality we enjoyed at his house. Indeed, I said, we both cherished the many pleasant and memorable evenings spent in the company of his family. I also expressed our gratitude for the motherly care extended to us by his wife. True, I admitted, during this short period of time, his daughter Eleanor and I had developed a mutual fondness for each other, and had it not been for the army, I would have considered it a privilege to marry her and become a member of his family. However, under the circumstances, I said, I was sure he would not expect me to marry his daughter and then go off to war in Europe. This, I pointed out, would not make any sense at all.

However, Mr. J. would not be easily discouraged, and he tried to convince me that there was still a solution to this problem. And so, looking me straight in the eye and watching my reaction, he said: "My dear boy, I cannot tell you how happy I am to hear that you are inclined to accept my proposition. But what I have in mind is not that you marry Eleanor and then go off to war in Europe. On the contrary, the idea is that, after marrying her, you stay on in this country. My plan is that you will be transferred from the anti-Semitic and nationalistic ranks of the Polish forces into the South African army, since both now come under the British Army's High Command. As a matter of fact, I have already made some inquiries in this direction, and found out that such a transfer could be effected, provided you ask for it officially, citing anti-Semitism in the Polish army."

I must say that during the short period of time I had known Mr. J., I found him to be an honest, frank, and upright person. Therefore, I was very much surprised, to say the least, that he should have come up with such a plan at all. For what he suggested was that I should join the South African army so that I could marry his daughter and be near home. I bluntly told him, without mincing words, that this was something I would not do. First, because of the debt I owed the Polish army, which, despite the anti-Semitism prevailing in its ranks, had enabled me to leave the Soviet Union. Even more importantly, because I felt an inner need to go and fight the Germans, who had so brutally killed off practically my whole family. I must have used very strong words, expressing my indignation at his plan, for Mr. J. made every effort to calm me down. To mitigate the effect of his suggestion, he now tried to use rational and other valid arguments to make me change my mind, and this is what he said:

"My friend, I can very well understand your desire and need for wanting to go and fight the Germans. But think for a moment what would happen if, God forbid, you should get killed in action, and there will be no one left to continue your family succession. If you would ask me, your first and foremost duty is to marry and have children. Only through them and their children will you be able to ensure your family's continuity." Looking serious and grim, Mr. J. continued: "Let those responsible for the war, whose families suffered no casualties, go and fight the Germans. Therefore, I again appeal to you to reconsider your stand, before making a final decision."

To say that Mr. J.'s forceful reasoning had left me unaffected would simply not be true. In fact, for the next few days, after the date of our departure was confirmed, I had to do some hard thinking. And in spite of mustering up all the arguments for and against Mr. J.'s proposition, I could not decide one way or the other. Then, all of a sudden, I recalled the famous advice once given by the late Mr. Bernard Baruch, elder statesman and presidential consultant on political and economic affairs in the U.S.A. When one of a couple asked for his counsel regarding their marital dispute, he said: "WHEN IN DOUBT, FOLLOW YOUR HEART!" And this is exactly what I did. Despite all the rational and other valid arguments used by Mr. J., in order to convince me to change my mind, and despite the widespread anti-Semitism in the Polish army, I decided to board the H.M.S. Anglia and, with the rest of the servicemen in my contingent, leave South Africa for Great Britain.

* * *

In the previous essay on the subject of intermarriage, I considered the reasons why gentile women, especially middle-class Christian women in western Europe, tend to marry Jewish males. I also remarked that this tendency is even more stunning, in view of the fact that throughout the centuries, various canon laws of the Catholic Church strictly forbade such mixed marriages. In this second essay on the same subject, I dealt with an opposite tendency, that is, one which discourages such mixed marriages. This time, however, it was the Jewish side that came out against it, as described in the above story of a typical Jewish family in South Africa.

Nevertheless, it is an undeniable fact, supported by statistical evidence, that since World War II, and especially after the establishment of the Jewish state in 1948, more and more gentile persons of both sexes make strenuous efforts to become Jewish. They do this in spite of the various obstacles they encounter in the pursuit of their goal. One of the main reasons for their difficulty is the fact that, unlike the Christian religion, as well as the majority of other faiths, the Jewish religion is probably one of the very few in the world that has no missionary aim of proselytizing others. If anything, just the opposite is true. And that is why Orthodox rabbis and the religious establishment they control, especially in Israel, place every possible obstacle in the way of would-be candidates for conversion, discouraging them from becoming Jewish.

A case in point that particularly alarmed the religious establishment in Israel, and even further intensified its negative attitude towards conversions, appeared in recent media reports received in the country. These warned that Israel was in danger of being swamped by tens of millions of new, rather unusual immigrants. According to these reports, the matter concerned tribesmen from the north-east Indian states of Manipur and Mizoram, natives of Pakistan, the Philippines, and Burma, as well as inhabitants of some other Third World countries, claiming to have Jewish roots. More specifically, all those prospective immigrants claimed to be descendants of the ancient Israelites, belonging to the tribe of Menashe, one of the Ten Lost Tribes which, according to the Bible, were exiled in 722 BCE.

Under the Law of Return enacted in 1950, following the trauma of the Holocaust and the establishment of the State of Israel, every person who claimed Jewish identity was almost automatically granted Israeli citizenship. However, due to the fact that some immigrants entered the country under false pretenses, it became necessary to establish detailed criteria for identifying "Who is a Jew," according to the law, and the benefits to which Jews are entitled under it. But this, in turn, raised the controversial question whether the definition of Jewish identity should be determined according to *Halakhah*, that is, principles of rabbinic jurisprudence, or by the mainstream secular establishment. And because the issue remains a major source of contention between the religious and secular parties of the country, the problem has not been resolved to this very day.

As already mentioned, the Jews of Europe have suffered religious persecutions, blood libels, murderous pogroms, as well as social and economic boycotts, throughout the centuries. All this took place for one – and only one – reason: Jews had refused to be converted to Christianity. And those who had become Christians, mostly by force, were later even rewarded for doing so. Some were offered positions in the civil service; others in local and national government; and still others found their place in the Church hierarchies of the countries of their abode.

Now we are witnessing a phenomenon in the opposite direction, namely: Many gentiles are eager to join the Jewish faith. This is in spite of the fact that, by doing so willingly and without any inducement, they expose themselves, whether consciously or not, to possible hardships and discrimination. Whatever their reasons for desiring to become Jewish, these gentiles are not only being discouraged by the rabbis of the religious establishment, but they neither expect nor are offered any reward for entering the Jewish faith, even if they manage to overcome all the obstacles in their way. A paradox? Call it what you will, but there is no doubt that there is much irony in this **asymmetrical situation.**

There are probably as many reasons as there are individuals and groups of people who desire to embrace the Jewish faith. However, one rather unusual motive I have heard merits mention here. It concerns a black man who attended a concert of Jewish religious music during a visit to Jerusalem. When asked by the man seated next to him why he was interested in this kind of music, his reply was that, apart from being Jewish, he was also a professor of music, with a special interest in *chazanut*, i.e., Jewish liturgical music. Greatly surprised at his reply, the Jerusalemite invited the professor to his house for a cup of coffee after the concert. During a long and friendly conversation, he turned to his guest and asked him bluntly: "Tell me, professor, tell me honestly, is it not enough for one to be black without carrying the additional burden of being a Jew?"

The professor, somewhat surprised by his host's question, replied: "Not at all! Not at all! You see," he explained, "In comparison with others, I find my Jewish co-religionists to be more forbearing and understanding of the difficulties black people encounter daily."

9 The Ill-Conceived Cleansing Slogans: "Poland For Poles!" And "Jews To Palestine!"

Anti-Semitism, widespread among Poles throughout the centuries, has always played an important role in the life of this Catholic nation, although with various degrees of intensity. Originally based on religious premises, it had spread out and penetrated into political and economic spheres, especially after World War I. However, to perceive the reasons for Polish anti-Semitism, especially during the interwar period, it is necessary to trace some details of its background history.

Poland as a sovereign state was reestablished as a result of World War I, and the unexpected collapse of the three partitioning powers. But the reborn state, aside from the territory of Congress Poland, although populated by ethnic Poles, also included areas in which minorities such as Ukrainians, Belorussians, Jews and Germans lived. The Treaty of Versailles provided, among other things, for the protection of the national rights of those minorities. Consequently, the Polish constitution stipulated that the state's ethnic minorities would be allowed to foster their national and cultural traditions and be protected from any discrimination due to religious, racial, or national differences. Within the framework of these principles, the Jews were recognized by the Polish state as a nationality with the explicit right to develop their own institutions on the basis of national autonomy.

In practical terms, however, the provisions of the Polish constitution concerning the national rights of the various minorities had not been fulfilled. If anything, the opposite was true. Far from preventing discrimination against non-Poles, the interwar policy of the newly reestablished state was to favor the ethnic Polish element at the expense of the various national minorities, and above all, at the expense of Jews, the only non-Christian ethnic group in the country.

As a result, Jews' activities towards the development and advancement of their own national life were either restricted or simply prohibited. This included various limitations imposed on the proper functioning of their *kehilot*, or local community organizations of the group's national autonomy. And so, instead of being the main organs of the advancement of Jewish national and cultural life in the country, the task of *kehilot* was relegated by the state to the role of merely dealing mainly with the religious life of the community. This was done by imposing a tight check on all their activities, and also by controlling their annual budgets.

Another important limitation imposed by the Polish state was the refusal to establish new Jewish schools, and the unwillingness of the Polish Ministry of Education to recognize the diplomas of existing Jewish secondary schools. Thus, a youth who attended such a school was, in effect, prevented from taking up university studies. And those who went to public schools instead were later restricted from entering any institution of higher learning, because of the *numerus clausus* limitation, applied to Jewish candidates. There were also other, similar restrictions specifically imposed on the Jewish population.

What most characterized the anti-Semitic policy of successive Polish governments during the interwar period, however, were the economic measures taken against the Jews. Apart from stringent government legislation and various restrictions imposed by local authorities, the state not only sanctioned, but actively encouraged the boycotting of Jewish enterprises, shops, as well as Jewish tradesmen, artisans and craftsmen. Characteristic of the anti-Jewish propaganda at the time, a boycott slogan widely circulated throughout the country read: "SWOJ DO SWEGO PO SWOJE" (To our own, for our own). It is important to emphasize here that, owing to this anti-Semitic policy of the Polish state, Jews were neither accepted into the Civil Service, nor could they be employed by any of the state-run monopolies, institutions, or enterprises. Apart from some merchants and industrialists, as well as most foreign-trained professionals, the vast majority of Jews was restricted to a narrow choice of livelihood opportunities, forced to engage as middlemen, traders, small shopkeepers and artisans. But even here, the Polish state pursued a policy of "cleansing" the country's commerce and trade of its Jewish citizens. This was done by encouraging and supporting the establishment of peasant cooperatives and other commercial units. The object was first to compete, and later to take over and engage in all the occupations held by Jews.

But apart from the negative attitude of the Polish state towards the national rights of the Jewish minority, there were also a number of organizations in the country whose political programs were specifically directed against the Jews. Among them, three particular parties gained considerable prominence, owing to their vigorous anti-Semitic activities. One of them, called "NARODOWA DEMOKRACJA" (ND), or "National Democracy," also referred to by its initials "Endeks," claimed to be the leading protagonist in the fight against the Jews. In its anti-Semitic attitude, the party struggled to preserve the Polish character of the country by fighting Jewish influence and competition. Another party, called "OBOZ NARODOWO-RADYKALNY" (ONR), or "National Radical Camp," was even more extreme in its attitude towards the Jewish minority. It modelled itself on the Nazi plan and adopted a program of action that criss-crossed with the anti-Semitic ideologies of Germany and Poland. And finally, the paramilitary anti-Semitic organization called "OBOZ ZJEDNOCZENIA NARODOWEGO" (OZON), or "Camp of National Unity," based on extreme nationalism, Catholicism, and anti-Semitism. The party propagated, amongst other things, the "Aryanization" of all professional organizations in the country, economic boycotts, and the destruction of Jewish property. Although successive Polish governments and the parties in question might have differed as to the exact way the anti-Jewish campaign should be fought, they agreed on pursuing three main measures, namely: anti-Jewish legislation, economic and social boycott, and ethnic cleansing.

All those measures, taken by successive Polish governments and the various parties during the interwar period, had one purpose, and one purpose only, namely to reduce the number of Jews in Poland to an absolute minimum, either by voluntary, or, if necessary, by forced emigration. It was during this period that the two notorious and previously mentioned anti-Jewish slogans were coined and widely propagated throughout the country, namely, "POLAND FOR POLES!" and "JEWS TO PALESTINE!" However, as often happens in the life of a nation, paradoxes cannot be avoided, as the following story will reveal.

Some time ago, I went, as I usually do on Wednesdays, to the local greengrocer to purchase our family's weekly supply of vegetables and fruit. But instead of the middle-aged Arab who used to attend to me, I found another man in his place. However, this new assistant – a young, tall, and intelligent looking man – somehow did not seem to fit the physical requirements of the job. Surprised, I asked the owner of the shop what had happened to his former employee. He gave me a meaningful look, and with a smile on his face answered that, because of all the troubles with the Arabs, he had decided to employ an academic from Poland instead. "By the way," the greengrocer asked me, "perhaps you speak Polish and could verify some information for me, as I am not sure I fully understood my new assistant? You see, apart from Polish, which I don't understand, the man speaks only some broken German."

"Certainly," I replied, and turned to the new assistant in his mother tongue.

From a short conversation with the young man, who was a qualified economist, I learned that, only about a month before, he had left Poland, together with his fiancee who was a university-trained teacher. She, too, found a job here, working as a nursemaid for the child of a young Israeli couple. It was because of unemployment, he explained, that they had decided to seek their fortunes abroad, as did many thousands of their compatriots for the same reason. But when I inquired why, instead of going to some neighboring European country, they chose faraway Israel, his reply was that at present the rate of unemployment in most of those countries was already very high. And even if they had been allowed to enter any European country, they would have had to compete with workers from Algeria, Turkey or Pakistan. Such a proposition, he added, would not have been worth their while.

On hearing his explanation, I was unable to check my sudden impulse and could not help exclaiming: "What a paradox! What a paradox!" And not without some hidden satisfaction I thought to myself: What a twist of a person's fate, to seek employment in a country and among people for whom the majority of his compatriots, and possibly he, too, felt nothing but contempt. "Did you know," I asked the young man, "that in pre-war Poland there were two widely circulated anti-Semitic slogans, 'Poland for Poles!' and 'Jews to Palestine!' And had it not been for the fact that many Jews, including myself, had decided to take this not so 'friendly advice' seriously," I continued, "we would now have no country of our own, and you would have no place to come and find a job."

Nevertheless, I assured the young Pole, that despite our recent not-so-happy history, he could expect friendly and proper treatment accorded to all foreign guests in our country. "I have no doubt about it whatsoever," answered the man, "in fact, from my short experience since my arrival, I can already confirm the friendly attitude of all the local people whom I have met. Those who come from Poland are especially very helpful, indeed. But why are you so offended by the slogan, 'Jews to Palestine!'" asked the man, "when your own government uses a somewhat similar phrase, calling on Jews to come to Israel?"

"Well," I replied, "don't you think that there is a basic difference between your country's derogatory and insulting slogan, urging Jews to leave Poland, accompanied by its various ways and means of actually driving them out of the country, and our positive call to our brethren the world over, inviting them to come and settle in Israel? Surely, any intelligent person could easily perceive this fundamental difference." The man tried to say something, but our conversation was interrupted by a customer who entered the shop.

Some time later, in a subsequent conversation with the young man regarding the economic situation in Poland, I observed that there was something basically wrong with his country's economy. Granted, I said, after a war there are always many problems and difficulties to overcome. But with the passage of time, one would expect conditions to stabilize, and then move towards gradual improvement. However, for some reason or other, Poland's economy seems to go the other way round, I observed. In the fifty years or so since the Second World War ended, things there have gone from bad to worse. "How do you account for that?" I asked the young man.

"Well, your assessment is quite right," he admitted, "but the reason for our problem is really simple. You see, after the war we had a number of Jewish ministers, in two or three successive governments. They were responsible for running the country's economy. But after they resigned from their positions, the situation started deteriorating to the point of our present state of affairs."

"Excuse me," I interjected, "if my memory does not fail me, your Jewish ministers never resigned on their own but were gradually ousted from their posts. In fact, this came about as a result of a sharp and prolonged campaign, which claimed, among other things, that there were too many Jews in your government." At this point we had to interrupt our dialogue again, because another customer had come into the shop.

After a short break, I resumed my conversation with the young Pole. I asked if he knew that after the Second World War, until the end of 1945, a total of 353 innocent Jews were reported murdered in Poland. This came about as a result of the population's anti-Semitic feelings, after the Germans had left the country. When confronted with this information, he simply answered that he never heard of such a great number of Jews having been killed by his own people.

But what he did say was that he heard of Poles who had helped Jews by hiding them from Germans at the risk of their own lives. I confirmed his assertion, but at the same time pointed out that of all the countries occupied by the Germans, the relative percentage of Jews saved in Poland was the smallest. According to Holocaust historians, the reason for this was the predominantly hostile attitude of the population, which was said to have rejoiced that Hitler appeared to be solving the Jewish question for them. In many cities, towns and villages, **some** people not only assisted in searching for hidden Jews, but joined the Nazis in torturing and even killing Jews as well. Therefore, it must be said that the rescue of Jews by some noble Poles dictated by humanitarian motives, or simply by materialistic considerations, was the exception rather than the rule.

After another break in our conversation, I resumed our dialogue again, and reminded him that in 1946, following the notorious pogroms in Krakov and Kielce, another 46 innocent Jews were killed, and many scores of others seriously wounded. Those affected were ex-partisans and other Jews who had succeeded in escaping slaughter by the Germans, and had come out of the forests and other hiding places to claim back their houses and other property. No wonder, I pointed out, that after such tragic events the remnants of an already greatly depleted Jewish population had left Poland for good.

"But how does one account for the fact that even now," I asked the man, "when there are practically no Jews left in the country, anti-Semitic feelings in Poland are still so very strong?"

"Well," he answered, "that is why the progressive part of our society is striving to curb the influence of the Church on our country's political life. It is this strong influence, especially on various right-wing and radical groups, that is responsible for their anti-Semitic actions. But they are definitely a minority in the country."

"Maybe so," I argued, "but how can one explain another fact that, despite all those tragic events, your present government is trying hard to woo Jewish businessmen, especially those in the United States and Israel, to come and help improve your country's economy?"

"Oh!" exclaimed the man, "that is a different matter altogether; that is business."

"And apart from that," added he smiling, "don't you know that there is an old and well-known Polish adage, 'Jak bida to do Zyda!' that is to say, 'When it is bad, you turn to the Jew!'"

Now, I ask you in all sincerity, is there any normal person who could possibly comprehend and explain this twisted, or rather perverted, logic of anti-Semitism?

Conclusion

In spite of the current officially changed attitude of the main Christian Churches in a number of western countries, the recent phenomenon of anti-Semitism around the world remains an ever-growing problem, especially in Europe. Jews are often discriminated against, intimidated, and even killed; Jewish graveyards are daily desecrated, and synagogues as well as offices of various Jewish institutions bombed or burned down. To this, one has to add the effects of a hostile press, numerous publications, books, films, plays, and other means of anti-Semitic propaganda, calling on the public of those countries to boycott the Jews socially and economically. In short, Judeophobia, in its various forms of activity, continues to inflict harm not only on individuals but also on entire Jewish communities.

In this context, it is important to stress the changing character of anti-Semitism, whilst its aims remain the same throughout the centuries. In the Middle Ages, as we have seen, it was based on Christian religious intolerance. With the advent of industrialization, anti-Semitism was interpreted as competition and envy of Jewish financial successes. But later, with the arrival of socialism and communism, Jews were accused of representing both the world's capitalism and international communism, even though one contradicts the other. And then again, with the establishment of the Jewish state, anti-Semitism conveniently appeared under the cover of anti-Zionism. However, the most paradoxical version of Judeophobia is its latest form, namely: anti-Semitism without Jews; for now it exists even in countries where the Jewish population has been almost completely eliminated, and in some places, never lived at all.

In such a state of affairs, the question to be asked is, what has gone wrong with all the measures taken by those concerned with combating anti-Semitism since World War II? When, after a thorough examination and assessment, the reasons for failure to combat anti-Semitism become known, another question may arise, namely whether the time has come to revise the present approach to dealing with this most perturbing and long-lasting social illness? It is outside the scope of this book to provide such an analysis, and to suggest better ways and means for fighting anti-Semitism more successfully. Nevertheless, some observations to this end might be helpful, especially with regard to the Christian world, with which this book is principally concerned. Of the three main bodies directly dealing with this endemic problem, namely, the Christian Churches, world Jewry, and the State of Israel, it is the Christian Churches' obligation that should be most pronounced in this struggle, for two reasons. First, because of the historical and moral responsibility for their main role in creating the problem in the first place; and secondly, even more importantly, because of the Churches' influence over an estimated 900,000,000 Christians in the world, some of whom continue to be actively engaged in pursuing the anti-Semitic ideology.

Unfortunately, owing to a combination of political and theological reasons, the Churches' official directives against Judeophobia are often disregarded, especially by the lower echelons of their hierarchy. And so, Catholic prelates, priests, and preachers in various countries are reluctant to abandon their anti-Semitic views and often continue preaching the Gospel in the old anti-Jewish spirit, even though this contradicts the Church's current official directives. They do so on various occasions, but especially during their sermons, lectures and various religious gatherings, thus fostering anti-Semitic tendencies among their religious followers.

A good example of how Church directives are not complied with is the recent opinion expressed by a Catholic priest on the subject of the notorious blood libel charges, levelled at the Jewish people for centuries. It was made on the 44th anniversary of the famous – or rather infamous – pogrom against Jews in the Polish town of Kielce in 1946. The reason for this pogrom, which became known only after a time, was a false rumor spread by anti-Semitic elements in the town, claiming that its Jewish citizens had kidnapped a Christian boy by the name of Henryk Blaszczyk and, after murdering him, used his blood for preparing *matzot*, unleavened bread, to be eaten during the Passover festival.

In 1990, almost half a century later, when a special program was prepared to be broadcast by Polish radio on the occasion of the Kielce pogrom's anniversary, a reporter interviewed a number of local citizens to find out their current views on the tragic events of 1946. Among those interviewed was a local priest. He was asked to give his opinion about the charge made against Jews that they use the blood of Christian children for their Passover rituals. And this is what the learned priest is said to have stated:

"In the Middle Ages such assumptions were possible, as in those days weaker nations (people) used the blood of other human beings; involved here is (the matter concerns) the blood of children (used) as extra food. But this could have been (could have occurred) in the Middle Ages. Today, after all, there are blood transfusions (available)."

Now, anybody familiar with the term *kosher* (here in the sense of purity) knows that Jewish dietary laws require complete removal of blood from any food, before it is prepared for consumption. How, then, could the shedding of blood, which is alien to the very nature of Judaism, be associated with such a primitive and evil notion? Unfortunately, beliefs like this are not isolated cases. Nevertheless, it must be most perturbing for any average person to learn that they are held not just by anybody, ignorant of the true facts, but by a Catholic priest, and in the twentieth century at that!

In this context, however, a more serious and fundamental question arises, namely, whether or not the said priest of Kielce was aware of and acquainted with the Papal Bulls of Innocent III, Innocent IV, Gregory X, and others, decreeing that all such blood libel charges made against the Jews were groundless. Most importantly, the question remains as to whether he was familiar with the "Nostra Aetate," the Vatican Council's Declaration of October 1965, on the subject of the Catholic Church's Relations to Non-Christian Religions? If these questions are answered in the negative, then one cannot but infer that there must be something wanting in the way the Holy See's directives are followed by the lower echelons of Church hierarchy. However, if the answer is affirmative, which I very much suspect is the case, then one cannot but come to the conclusion that, as far as the Jews and their religion are concerned, Church directives are left to be accommodated, and freely interpreted by any individual clergyman, as he thinks appropriate. Otherwise, how can one explain the Kielce priest's views, which are contradictory to the official directives of the Catholic Church?

And for the benefit of all those who are not familiar with the above-mentioned "Nostra Aetate" declaration of October 1965, here are some relevant and important excerpts from it:

"The Church repudiates all (kinds of) persecutions against any people. Mindful of her common patrimony (heritage) with the Jews, and motivated by the Gospel's spiritual love, and not by any political considerations, the Church deplores (condemns) the hatred, persecutions, and displays of anti-Semitism directed against the Jews at any time and from any source." Further, the said declaration states: "Jesus, his Apostles and part of His disciples, were born in the Jewish nation (were Jews)." Jesus employed teaching methods analogous (similar) to those used by the rabbis (Jewish law teachers of the day). Now, if that is the case, then is it at all feasible even to think that Jesus, born as a Jew of a Jewish mother, would use human blood for Jewish religious

**practices, before the advent of Christianity? The Holy
See's declaration also states: "Spiritual bonds and
historical references (relations) that link the Church
with Judaism, demand of us to condemn
anti-Semitism, and any form of discrimination, being
contrary to the very spirit of Christianity."**

From all that has been said so far, the only reasonable
conclusion one can make is to find ways and means to bridge
the gap between the Churches' official directives against
anti-Semitism, and their successful implementation by all
those concerned. This applies in particular to the lower
echelons of the Churches' hierarchy, active in various countries
throughout the Christian world. True, for some years now, the
Churches themselves are beset by many problems of their own,
such as priests' celibacy, ordination of women, liberation
theology, birth control, homosexuality, etc. But all these
problems, important as they are, should in no way distract the
Churches from pursuing their long-overdue efforts to eliminate
the continuous harm resulting from Christian anti-Semitism.

It must be emphasized that the decision as such by the
Catholic Church merely to remove anti-Semitic passages from
prayers, school textbooks, and other religious instruction
material, will not by itself suffice. To be effective, it must be
supplemented with, and backed up by, revised teaching
programs for schools, colleges, universities and, above all,
institutions for training future priests, ministers, and other
clergymen. Subjects such as an unbiased history of the Jewish
people, the Holocaust and its lessons, the revival of Israel, and
other related topics, should be included in their studies. In

addition, lectures, seminars, and regular meetings between Christian and Jewish community representatives would help minimize any possible friction between them and foster a better understanding between Christians and Jews. With this object in mind, particularly good results could be achieved by the effective use of the various means of mass communication, especially the electronic media. However, to make sure that all these corrective measures are actually carried out, a special coordinative mechanism on a national level should be set up in each country.

A good example of an effort towards achieving this end is the decision recently taken by the Polish government. Anxious to combat anti-Semitism in a more effective way, it established a special body to deal with every aspect of the problem. Its National Council of Christians and Jews consists of Church leaders, educators and politicians, as well as representatives of the country's people themselves. Basing their activities on the principle that anti-Semitism must be fought continuously, these participants cooperate and coordinate their work with the government, the Church, and other institutions of the country. Among their tasks is to eliminate, from Church and government official texts, any anti-Semitic passages affecting Jews and Judaism. In addition, they keep under constant review the country's existing legal measures in respect of anti-Semitic crimes, and suggest new laws to prevent anti-Jewish agitation.

Should the Polish example of dealing with this endemic problem prove successful – and there is no reason why it should not, provided the matter is seriously dealt with by all parties concerned – it could serve as a model for other countries to follow. The relative merit of such a solution, as adopted by the Polish government, lies in the fact that it is not imposed from the outside, but devised and operated by those concerned themselves, having taken into account the particular character, conditions, and other factors affecting the people and the country in question.

Few issues are more complex and more bound up with tension and misunderstanding than the question of relations between Christians and Jews. Though the present process of changing Christian attitudes towards the Jews and Judaism is too slow and definitely far from being satisfactory, it would be folly to expect that two thousand years of anti-Semitism can be easily eradicated by some magical and quick solution. Centuries of biased indoctrination by both Church and school have resulted in deeply rooted anti-Jewish feelings in Christian society. And so, it required two extraordinary and significant events to shake Christian hearts and minds, in order to start a process of changing this attitude.

One event was the terrible tragedy of the Holocaust, in which over six million – or one third of the Jewish people – were so brutally massacred; and the other event was the establishment of an independent Jewish state. The first resulted in the initiation of a process of rectifying centuries of oppression, persecution, degradation, and social injustice suffered by the Jews. The second brought about the creation of a homeland in which the Jews have redeemed their national freedom, and can live in dignity, pride, security and protection. It remains now for the Christian world to pursue with increased vigor, determination and effectiveness the process embarked

on, of rectifying its negative attitude towards the Jewish people, who live among them, and who continue contributing to their mutual welfare and to the development of the countries whose citizens they happen to be.

Notes

1. **The Augustinian Doctrine** claimed to be based on true religious principles of instruction and teaching, as codified and laid down anew in 1602. It reinforced the notion that the Jews are a wandering, rejected, accursed, and apostate people, blind to any spiritual meaning. The Oxford English Dictionary on Historical Principles (1987).

2. **The Third Lateran (11th Ecumenical) Church Council,** summoned by Pope Alexander III in 1179, dealt with relations between Jews and Christians. Canon 26 imposed many prohibitions and limitations on Jews living in Christian lands. J. G. Grayzel, Church and the Jews (1966), and Encyclopaedia Judaica, Volume 5, Lateran Councils.

3. **The Fourth Lateran (12th Ecumenical) Church Council,** summoned by Pope Innocent III in 1215, dealt with various heresies. Canons 67 and 68 reinforced and extended a number of previously enacted anti-Jewish laws by the Catholic Church. J.G. Grayzel, Church and the Jews (1966), and Encyclopaedia Judaica, Volume 5, Lateran Councils.

4. **The Second Vatican Council (1962-65),** initiated by Pope John XXIII, dealt with the attitude of the Catholic Church toward Judaism. The Declaration: "Nostra Aetate" (In Our Time), formulated the position of the Church vis-a-vis the non-Christian religions. The Declaration was officially promulgated on October 28, 1965. J. D. Parkes, Conflict of the Church and Synagogue (1966), and Encyclopaedia Judaica, Volume 5, Vatican Councils I and II.

5. **The Sikorski-Maisky Agreement** between the Polish government-in-exile and the Soviet Union was concluded in London on July 30, 1941. It provided for the release of all Polish citizens from Soviet prisons and forced labor camps, and the formation of the Polish army on Soviet territory. Josef Galinski, Poland in the Second World War (1985).

6. **The Ribbentrop-Molotov Agreement** (Non-Aggression Pact) between Germany and the Soviet Union was concluded on August 23, 1939. Its secret paragraphs provided for the division of Eastern Europe into German and Soviet spheres of influence. Josef Galinski, Poland in the Second World War (1985).

7. **Justinian Laws** are based on various decrees issued by different rulers in ancient times. Assembled and introduced by Justinian, the Byzantine Emperor, in 565, they were later codified and adopted throughout the Roman Empire. The Oxford English Dictionary on Historical Principles (1987).

8. **Canon Laws** (ecclesiastical laws) contain decrees or edicts, laid down by the conferences of various statutory Church Councils, presided over and confirmed by highest ecclesiastical authority. The Oxford English Dictionary on Historical Principles (1987).

9. **The estimated numbers of Jews saved from Nazi extermination** are as follows: In France up to 200,000, or one third of the Jewish population; in Belgium 26,000, or 45 percent; in Holland 16,000, or 11 percent; in Italy 35,000, or 80 percent; in Austria and Germany 5,000, or 2 percent; in Poland 25,000 to 40,000, or up to 1.5 percent; in Hungary 200,000, or 26 percent of the country's Jewish population. Mordecai Paldiel, Gentile Rescuers of Jews During the Holocaust, Ktav Publishing House, Inc., New York (1989).

10. **The number of anti-Semitic incidents worldwide in 1991** increased by 35 percent over the previous year (no figures given). The number of anti-Semitic attacks in 1992, increased from 1879 to 1990 in 1993. The above figures were officially disclosed during the First International Conference on anti-Semitism, sponsored by the World Jewish Congress held in Brussels in 1993.

Further Reading

- Almog, Shmuel (ed.), Anti-Semitism Through the Ages, Oxford, 1988.

- Arendt, Hannah, Anti-Semitism, New York, 1968.

- Berger, David (ed.), History and Hate: The Dimension of Anti-Semitism, Philadelphia, 1986.

- Brockway, A., Learning Christology Through Dialogue with Jews, 1985.

- Byrnes, Robert, Anti-Semitism in Modern France, New Brunswick, 1950.

- Cohen, Jeremy, The Friars and the Jews: Evolution of Medieval Anti-Judaism, Ithaca, 1982.

- Cohn-Sherbok, D., Holocaust Theology, Lamp, 1989.

- Croner, Helga (ed.), Stepping Stones to Further Jewish-Christian Relations, New York, 1985.

- Curtis, Michael (ed.), Anti-Semitism in the Contemporary World, Boulder, 1986.

- Davies, A.T. (ed.), Anti-Semitism and the Foundation of Christianity, New York, 1987.

- Dinnerstein, Leonard, Anti-Semitism and the American Experience, New York, 1987.

- Ettinger, Shmuel, Anti-Semitism in the Modern Age, Tel Aviv, 1978 (in Hebrew).

- Fontette, François (ed.), Historia Antysemityzmu, Wydawnictwo Siedmiorog, 1992 (in Polish).

- Friedman, Theodore (ed.), Anti-Semitism in the Soviet Union, its Roots and Consequences, New York, 1984.

- Gager, John, The Origins of Anti-Semitism: Attitudes Towards Judaism in Pagan and Christian Antiquity, Oxford, 1985.

- Gilbert, Martin, The Holocaust, London, 1986.

- Glassman, Bernard, Anti-Semitic Stereotypes Without Jews; Images of Jews in England 1290-1700, Detroit, 1973.

- Hay, Malcolm, The Roots of Christian Anti-Semitism, New York, 1981.

- Holms, Colin, Anti-Semitism in British Society, New York, 1979.

- Isaak Jules, Has Anti-Semitism Roots in Christianity? New York, 1961.

- Kersten, Krystyna, Polacy, Zydzi, Komunizm, Anatomia Polprawd, 1939-68, Niezalezna Oficyna Wyd. Warszawa, 1991 (in Polish).

- Klein, Charlotte, Anti-Judaism in Christian Theology, London, 1975.

- Korey, William, The Soviet Cage: Anti-Semitism in Russia, New York, 1973.

- Kushner, Tony, The Persistence of Prejudice: Anti-Semitism in British Society During the Second World War, Manchester, 1989.

- Langmuir, Gavin, History, Religion and Anti-Semitism, Berkeley, 1990.
- Lendvai, Paul, Anti-Semitism Without Jews: Communist Eastern Europe, New York, 1971.
- Lewis, B., Semites and Anti-Semites: An Inquiry into Conflict and Prejudice, New York, 1986.
- Littel, Franklin, The Crucifixion of the Jews, New York, 1975.
- Litvinoff, B., The Burning Bush: Anti-Semitism and World Jewry, London, 1989.
- Mehlman, Geoffrey, Legacies of Anti-Semitism in France, Minneapolis, 1983.
- Parkes, James, Anti-Semitism, London, 1963.
- Pawlikowsky, John, Christ in the Light of Christian-Jewish Dialogue, New York, 1982.
- Perlmutter, N. and R., The Real Anti-Semitism in America, New York, 1982.
- Quinley, Harold, and Clock, Charles, Anti-Semitism in America, New Brunswick, 1983.
- Sandmel, Samuel, Anti-Semitism in the New Testament, Philadelphia, 1978.
- Sartre, Jean-Paul, Anti-Semite and Jew, New York, 1976.
- Seidel, Gill, The Holocaust Denial: Anti-Semitism, Racism and the New Right, London, 1986.
- Thoma, Clemens, A Christian Theology of Judaism, New York, 1980.
- Valentin, Hugo, Anti-Semitism, London, 1986.

- Weinberg, Mayer, Because They Were Jews: A History of Anti-Semitism, New York, 1986.

- Wiacek, Tadeusz, Zabic Zyda: Kulisy I Tajemnice Pogromu Kieleckiego, Oficyna Wyd. Temax, Krakow, 1992 (in Polish).

- Wistrich, Robert, Anti-Semitism: The Longest Hatred, London, 1991.

- Wistrich, Robert, Anti-Zionism and Anti-Semitism in the Contemporary World, London, 1992.